# "THE **R** FATHER"

## 14 Ways to **R**espond to the Lord's Prayer

# "THE R" FATHER

## 14 Ways to Respond to the Lord's Prayer

MARK HART

Published by The Word Among Us Press
9639 Doctor Perry Road
Ijamsville, Maryland 21754
wau.org
14 13 12 11 10   1 2 3 4 5
ISBN: 978-1-59325-174-1

Cover design by Faceout Studio, faceoutstudio.com

Made and printed in the United States of America

Library of Congress Cataloging-in-Publication Data
Hart, Mark, 1973-
   The "R" Father : 14 ways to respond to the Lord's prayer / Mark Hart.
      p. cm.
   Includes bibliographical references.
   ISBN 978-1-59325-174-1
   1. Lord's prayer—Criticism, interpretation, etc. I. Title. II. Title: Our Father.
   BV230.H425 2010
   248.3'2088282--dc22
                              2010004425

To my daughters, Hope, Trinity, and Faith—
I pray that your view of our heavenly Father will never be
tainted by the failures of your earthly father.
I pray that you know his love through my love.
I pray that you'll trust me when I tell you to trust him.
I pray you'll live your life for God our Father.
I pray you'll always know how much he and I love you.
And always remember: No matter what life throws at you . . .
live for heaven.

And to my wife, Melanie—
I love you with everything I am . . . and still he loves you more.
What an amazing Father, huh?

# Contents

# Introduction

ountless books have been written about the Lord's Prayer, most by people far more qualified than I. There is one reason that I prayerfully agreed to write this book: The Lord's Prayer has literally changed my life. I trust it can change yours too. If you want to learn how to pray, this is where you start. If you want to deepen your prayer life, the Lord's Prayer is where you begin again.

In the Lord's Prayer, we are given a glimpse into the very heart of God. In this prayer, spanning just a few verses of the gospel, Jesus teaches us *how to pray* by simultaneously teaching *what to pray (for)*. This is the not the Lord simply teaching us what to say or how to say it. This is our Savior teaching us how to think, how to love, and how to receive God's love. Jesus is offering us a heart transplant. We have the opportunity to trade in our hard and wounded hearts for his compassionate and Sacred Heart.

The Lord's Prayer is simultaneously many things and one thing. It is the perfect prayer "from the perfect Pray-er."[1] It is adoration. It is petition. It is a reordering and reprioritizing so that we know what's most important. It is an invitation to a deeper relationship. It begs and celebrates God for his grace. It rejoices in the Father's fidelity. It promises eternity and offers hope to humanity. The Lord's Prayer expresses the totality of what it means to love and the summation of what it means to be a true child of God.

Jesus gave us these words after being asked about his own prayer life. The Master was always retreating—to the mountain, to the seashore, to the garden. Everywhere Christ traveled, he had his favorite places of solitude for peace and conversation with the Father. For Jesus, prayer was never an obligation or daily ritual; prayer was his very breath. His personal prayer paved the way for what we now consider a communal one, and that is the point: The Lord's Prayer is both private and public, both personal and ecclesial. It comes straight from the body of Christ for the body of Christ.

### Why this "R" Father?

This book is not intended to be a deeply theological treatise on the Lord's Prayer. This is not an exegetical study on the Scriptures. Consider it a reintroduction, a dusting off of a family heirloom, a quick spring cleaning for the soul. On the pages that follow, you'll be immersed in the timeless wisdom offered in the Scriptures, Church writings, and the saints, and you'll be able to draw some lessons from the humbling personal experiences of this saint-in-the-making.

I grew up as a cradle Catholic, vigilantly learning my prayers and reciting them with discipline. However, even as I got older, my devotion was rooted in ritual, not relationship. Prayer occupied a place in my schedule but not in my heart. I had no idea of the wisdom, peace, and power of the sacraments or prayer. The Church offered me Niagara Falls, but I saw only a leaking faucet. I had grown up physically and mentally, but spiritually I had remained a child.

It wasn't until I was charged with the catechesis and spiritual upbringing of young people that I began to see how shallow my own prayer life truly was. Then I discovered that I could deepen my prayer life by turning to the prayer that Jesus taught us. By meditating and reflecting on the Lord's Prayer, I've gained a new-found respect and deep-seated love for this prayer and all that it has shown me about our Father in heaven.

The Lord's Prayer is an invitation into a daily relationship. The fact is that if we go to bed underwhelmed by God's love, we weren't as present to him as he was to us that day. This prayer orders our priorities right from the beginning: God first, us second; worship before petition. If our prayer is only about petition (what we have to say), we lose the worship, the adoration, the thanksgiving, and the ability to discern what God is saying to us. In short, we lose the relationship.

Unfortunately, the one-way, shorthanded, and sporadic communication that exists in our social-networking culture can

> **Because the Lord's Prayer is so familiar to us, we risk reciting it instead of praying it.**

deafen us spiritually. And because the Lord's Prayer is so familiar to us, we risk reciting it instead of praying it. My hope and prayer for you is that this book will help you develop a deeper, two-way relationship with the Father, Son, and Holy Spirit, as well as a renewed love and devotion for this prayer that Jesus taught us.

Is there a danger in reading this book? If you read it and rededicate yourself to this prayer, your life is going to change. Things might get better quickly. Things might get "worse" before they get better. The irresistible love of God is gentle, not forceful. He will come into your life in ways you are probably not expecting.

The only thing the devil wants less than for me to write this book is for you to read it. I offer that sentence in confidence, not because I believe my words to be so insightful and eloquent, but because I know the Lord's Prayer to be powerful. The devil doesn't want you anywhere near the Father or the prayer that leads you deeper into his heart. The evil one has our modern culture right where he wants it—untrusting, and feeling as if the only way to survive is by our own knowledge and know-how. Jesus Christ says differently.

As children, we were told that school is about the three "R"s: reading, writing and 'rithmetic. In this book we're going to take a look at a series of "R"s too—fourteen, to be exact. We are going to take Jesus' words, line by line, to see what we are really *praying* in the Lord's Prayer. In contemplating each of these fourteen "R"s, you will be given ideas on how to respond to the Lord's Prayer each day, so that it might come more to life in your life.

Now let us pray.

Mark Hart

# CHAPTER ONE

# "Our"

## An Invitation into RELATIONSHIP

I vividly recall my Little League days: a dozen hyperactive young boys wearing plastic-mesh baseball caps with iron-on letters, scrambling around the dugout and infield in search of not a team win but individual glory (and eventually snow cones). I was a left-handed batter, which did not bode well for me.

In professional baseball, southpaws offer a team an advantage, a strategic tool that has game-changing implications. In the league of little boys, however, left-handed batters are a scourge. I quickly learned that pinpoint accuracy and prepubescent pitchers do not coincide. I got hit by the ball . . . a lot!

So bad was the pitching that my coach actually began encouraging me to "lean in" to the pitch rather than to swing at it. At least, he reasoned, I would get a walk. As the hitter involved in this equation, I disagreed.

"Lean in, Mark," my coach would shout exuberantly, to my dismay. I would look at him quizzically, pretending not to understand why he would encourage such an act of self-mortification. All the more urgently, he would plead: "*Lean in, Mark! There's no 'I' in team.*"

In those moments, my eleven-year-old conscience faced a challenging question, a social dilemma that only intensified in the years to come: Am I willing to sacrifice my body for the good of the many?

My answer then was "Nope!" I didn't lean in. I got the hit and was later tagged out. It didn't really matter. We were already down by ten runs and lost the game due to the mercy rule. "Our" team lost but "I" won. I got my snow cone—blueberry, if my memory serves me correctly.

### Taking a step back before we move forward

When it comes to our modern world, one might say that the "I's" have it. Look no further than Facebook or the aptly named MySpace. These online "communities" are rooted less in the "we" than they are in the "me." Twitter is even more self-focused, aiming only at what we have to tell others about ourselves in 140 characters or less. Many of us prefer the video-game version of reality—a "Wii" with two distinct "i's." Ironically, while typing that sentence, I heard my iPhone ringing. Thank you, Lord; I'll consider that a confirmation of my point.

Dietitians and trainers warn us about being out of shape, but modern culture is not in bad shape so much from what it consumes as from being so consumed with self. In the Little League of life, we're more concerned about our own batting average than about doing what's best for our team.

How, then, does this relate to this "R" Father? In order to truly understand the "our" in Our Father, we must look at the second word so that we can fully comprehend the first. These words are about **relationship**: the relationship between Father and child, yes, but more specifically, between God and his child*ren*.

Once we widen our scope beyond the first word—"our"—to the address, "Our Father," we quickly see it in context, as an important series of points that our Lord makes. If God is the

Father, then we are *all* his children; we're all connected as brothers and sisters in the Lord's Prayer. The Our Father is not merely a private prayer between you and your God or between one child and his or her divine "Daddy." This is the prayer of a family, a prayer between God the Father and every one of his children. The Our Father is no longer just personal but also corporate; the prayer is intimate but also communal. In this way too, the Sacrifice of the Mass really mirrors the Lord's Prayer; it is both personal and communal in its focus and guides our worship back to the Father in one collective breath.

### The bond is bigger than the building

Have you ever stopped to consider why there are over six billion people on one planet and not one person on six billion different planets? Couldn't God have done it that way too? Why put us all together on this spinning blue marble hurling through the solar system? Why force us to live and work together and get along? What is the Father trying to teach his children?

> We are more than creatures; we are children. We are in this together.

We are more than bodies; we are souls. We are more than creatures; we are children. We are in this together. We are one *creation* under God, indivisible. The fact is that all are created by God in his divine image (see Genesis 1:26-27). This truth cannot be overstated. God didn't just establish a **relationship** with us personally; he established and ordained us in **relationships** *with one another*.

If for no other reason (and there are plenty we'll cover), this should be enough to lead us to Mass on Sundays. People who say, "I feel closer to God by going into nature and communing with a tree" ought to do that—at some *other point* during the 167 remaining hours each week. As for that hour on Sunday, the very least we can offer as a member of God's family is to act like it.

The Church is more than a building. The body of Christ is made of living stones (1 Peter 2:4-5; see 1 Corinthians 12:27). Like Christ, the Church is both human and divine. The Church is human in that we are the people in need of redemption, members of God's family who have all been touched by sin. The Church is also divine: It is the bride of Christ, perfect in teaching and guided by the Holy Spirit. The Church is the primary sacrament from which all others flow (see *Catechism of the Catholic Church*, 774–76).

It's in this Church, this body of believers, that grace and sin collide, that perfection kisses imperfection. In ancient times it was only at the Mass that master and servant were equals; even if for only a short time, love, peace, fellowship, and equality were

> **It's in this Church, this body of believers, that grace and sin collide.**

extended to one another. Sunday worship knew no class system (Galatians 3:28); the only credentials necessary for admission were sin and an ardent desire for the new life available only in Christ (see Galatians 2:20; 2 Corinthians 5:15).

It is as the Church, more perfectly than anywhere else in existence, that we acknowledge the "our" of our existence. Steeped in a collective **relationship** as children of our one heavenly Father, we share a family name, an eternal bond, a universal kinship, and a divine heritage. There is a public persona to the body of Christ, which means that my actions and sins, no matter how seemingly private, affect and influence every one of my brothers and sisters. For that reason, Christ warns us of the need to seek personal holiness (Matthew 5:48), to love one another (John 13:34-35), and to watch out for one another (Romans 12:10-16; Ephesians 4:32; 1 Thessalonians 5:11). We are in this together.

Christ came not just to redeem us but to restore us to proper **relationship** with God *and with one another.* His healings of the leper (Matthew 8:2-4) or the woman with a hemorrhage (Mark 5:29-34) were not just about healing; they were about restoring the outcast to full community. His encounters with the woman caught in adultery (John 8:2-11) or the Samaritan woman at the well (John 4:4-42) were not merely to demonstrate the dignity he saw in women but also to broad the invitation to *everyone*, sinner and non-Jew alike, into a deeper, universal **relationship** with one another as the children of God, the body of Christ.

### The law of love has two parts

We can never forget that the "Greatest Commandment" has two parts to it. It's not merely to love the Lord your God with all your heart, mind, soul, and strength (see Matthew 22:37-38); it includes a second (not secondary) command that reminds us of the **relationship.** "Love your neighbor as yourself" (22:39), we are told. If we *fail to see* God in our neighbor, much less love him, we have failed to love God himself (see 25:40). In this way, when we fail to love others, we are breaking the first commandment to love God. How often do we confess that failure? Speaking for myself, I don't view my neighbors in this light nearly enough.

In praying "Our" Father, we are praying not only *with* but also *for* our brothers and sisters in Christ. Jesus is giving us more than an invitation to a **relationship** with his Father in this catechesis on prayer. He's giving us an introduction to our greater family—the true body of Christ—and an initiation into a new way of living.

This is yet another reason why a **relationship** with Mary and the saints is so necessary and invaluable in our own growth as Christians. Asking others to pray for us is a sign of humility and trust. Beseeching the intercessory prayer of the communion of saints—those brothers and sisters in the faith who have gone before us and finished the race (1 Corinthians 9:24-27; Hebrews 12:2)— is the only way we can be in full and total **relationship** with the body of Christ. How shortsighted it would be of us as Christians to think that our full communion with the body of Christ would

## True communion with Christ necessitates a relationship with all people.

stop with those who are still confined to their earthly, sinful existence. How small-minded it would be *not* to incorporate the souls of those who are far more fully alive than we are.

True communion with Christ necessitates a **relationship** with all people, believers and nonbelievers, whether past, present, or future; we are all inexorably linked by God. We are especially linked to the communion of saints by the upper room and the cross of Calvary. Mass is the greatest warm-up to becoming part of the communion of saints, for at Mass we are worshipping alongside the saints and angels, seeking the grace we need to live lives of joyful abandonment to God as they did.

### The equality of the relationship

Adam and Eve had it so good in Eden. All their needs were met. They had been given a priceless gift that could be neither bought nor earned: the gift of divine sonship. They were God's children.

What is even more amazing is that the gift of Adam and Eve's sonship cannot begin to compare to the sonship of God's eternal Son, Jesus Christ. Jesus' sonship is infinitely more glorious than Adam's sonship for this very simple reason: Christ (the eternal Son) is God! Through our baptism this is now "our" sonship; we are brought into this divine sonship of Christ by Christ himself. This is where the "our" comes from when we address the Father.

Stop and consider what we are being taught about this **relationship** with God from the first word of the Lord's Prayer: Our heavenly Father has given us a gift even more powerful and glorious than the gift he gave Adam and Eve at the very beginning. God gave us himself—Jesus. And Jesus himself gives us to his Father.[2] We are declared and made divinely adopted sons and daughters of God (1 John 3:1). As the new Adam (1 Corinthians 15:22, 45), Christ rights our **relationship** again. Where Adam failed, Jesus succeeded. Where Adam sinned, Jesus obeyed (Luke 22:42). Where Adam died in sin, Christ rose to life in glory (Romans 6:4). And the life that Adam lost in sin, the eternal Son has given us even more abundantly in love.

This love, given so freely (1 John 4:8, 19), reminds us of God's divine identity, as well as our own eternal destiny as one family. Our family is imperfect, a mixed bag of holy and unholy; our family tree is a wide assortment of fruit (and nuts), with every branch proudly displaying fruit—the good, the bad, and the ugly. And through all this painful reality, God does not play favorites. God loves the atheist as much as the priest, the prostitute as much as the virgin, the drug dealer as much as the saint. Ponder that for a moment. God's love is not fickle; God's love is fatherly. God, as perfect unconditional Love, cannot put conditions on his love. God cannot pick a favorite son or daughter in his body (the body of Christ) anymore than you can pick a favorite cell in your physical body.

## Responding to This Petition

### Reviewing "our" viewpoint

If we do not see the culture of "I" from which we need to break free, we'll never be a true Church, and the Mass (which is a liturgy, translated as a "public work") will continue to be the private prayer of hundreds of individuals who just so happen to be gathered in one place. If we are not willing to reach out, literally and figuratively, and allow those worshipping around us to walk with us in our brokenness, then the whole point of the incarnation has been lost.

This **relationship** between you and God (through Christ) and between you and others is the foundation to the rest of the Lord's Prayer. It is also the foundation of Christ's Church and ought to be the foundation of our lives as Christians. We are baptized into the family of the Holy Trinity (Matthew 28:19-20). He uses this family relationship, offered through our baptism, to invite others (the unbaptized) into his family. It's through this lens of family, this **relationship** with God and with one another, that we move deeper into the Lord's prayer and, more specifically, into our Father's heart.

## Questions for Reflection and Discussion

1. Does an impartial look at your day or week reflect an "I-focused" or an "our-focused" approach to your life?

2. Does your time at church demonstrate a desire to grow in community—an awareness of and appreciation for the "our" of God's family—or a desire to remain in solitude and relative anonymity?

3. In your personal faith walk, which is more difficult: loving your neighbor or loving yourself?

4. What is one concrete thing you can do in the coming day or week to really reach out of your comfort zone (from the "I" to the "our") and acknowledge the presence of Christ in the people around you?

# CHAPTER TWO

# "Father"

## A Title of Divine REVELATION

I magine that you receive an unexpected call telling you that your father has died. The next few days are a flurry of activity involving flights, funeral arrangements, and phone calls. Upon returning to your parents' home, you head to the attic to retrieve some of your father's personal effects for a memorial service. While there, you spot an old trunk with his name etched across the front, so you stoop down to investigate its contents.

A wealth of treasures greets you. You unload box after box of pictures and letters. Digging deeper, you discover journals and other keepsakes from your father's early childhood and through his young adult years. Quickly you discover a younger version of your father, recognizable but somehow "different" than you remember him. You dust off a photograph of him in a hospital room. The picture is yellow but discernible—he's holding a baby in the photo, and you realize that it's you.

As you leaf through a journal penned in your father's own handwriting, you're left almost speechless. You read of his fears for your future. You grow in awareness and appreciation for his sacrifices, difficult personal sacrifices so that you might have an education. You are shocked to learn of his disciplined and devoted prayer life and how, daily, he asked God to protect and guide you.

The hardened outer image of your father is being smashed and recreated into something new. How had you not known this part of your father? How had you not seen it before? At what point had your relationship stopped growing? Why had you allowed it to become so impersonal and cold? Perhaps it was your pride, not his, that had strained the relationship.

You are filled with memories of all the times your father tried to reach out to you, but you were too busy. You now realize that your father hadn't grown away from you; you had grown away from him. Your vision now clear, you come to terms with the reality of your father's love, a divinely appointed **revelation** that you had not been prepared to deal with.

Does this picture resonate with you at all? Has your relationship (or lack thereof) with your earthly father had an effect (up

## Has your relationship with God the Father grown at all cold or impersonal?

until now) on your relationship with your Father in heaven? Has your relationship with God the Father grown at all cold or impersonal? How about with your earthly father? Is that relationship all God hopes it to be?

### *Oh Father, where art thou?*

What kind of Father is God, anyway? Often times we struggle in intimacy with our heavenly Father because we project feelings of abandonment or ambivalence that we may have had toward our earthly fathers. And those feelings, though valid, are not the reality of God the Father's love for you. That being the case, before we can get to our Father in heaven, we need to briefly take a look at the modern state of fatherhood on earth.

It's been reported that in America, 34 percent of our young people go to sleep at night in a house where there is no father.[3] Our culture is reeling from a true epidemic of fatherlessness. This statistic is in no way given to make assertions, lay blame, or judge anyone; as both a stepfather and a birth father, I know well the challenges of blended families and parenthood. It does, however, present an increasingly dismal picture of paternal intimacy. And this fatherlessness is not reserved in any way to divorced, blended, or single-parent families—far from it. Many of the teens that I have encountered in the past two decades of youth ministry struggle more with an emotional lack of presence from their fathers than a physical one. They share a roof with their fathers but little else.

So why even address these issues in this chapter on the "Father"? This book is about our heavenly Father, not earthly fathers, right? However, until we redefine our natural assumptions of what a father is and is not, we cannot receive the **revelation** that Christ offers us in his prayer *to our heavenly Father*. Unless we deprogram our concept of father, the Holy Spirit cannot reprogram it.

### Revelation is more than a book

Earthly fathers—even St. Joseph!—will always fall short of the perfect love of our heavenly Father. That being said, *Christ still gives us this term "Father"* in this prayer. He didn't refer to him as Master, Creator, or Potter, as others had so many times before in the Old Testament (Isaiah 51:22; Jeremiah 3:14; Sirach 32:13 and 33:13; Isaiah 40:28; Isaiah 64:7-8). And while Christ is the only person to walk the earth who had the literal "right" to address the God of the universe as Father, he didn't have to teach *us* to pray that way. Yet he chose to **reveal** the Father to us as our own Father. Christ **reveals** to us a true Father, a Daddy he invites us to call "Abba" (Mark 14:36).

The idea of God as a father was not completely unknown to the people in Jesus' time. Scripture scholar Dr. Scott Hahn insightfully reminds us that "other religions have invoked their gods as father, but they have used the title only in a metaphorical sense— meaning that their god is *like* a father, because he begets them, guides them, and provides for them."[4] What Jesus **reveals** to us is that God is a father because of who he is, not merely because of what he does. It is not the "providing for the children" that makes God our Father; it is his essence—his very nature of love— that makes him our Father (1 John 4:19).

> **Many of us are conditioned to view fatherhood as provider first and as nurturing parent a distant second.**

In many homes fatherhood is seen exclusively through the lens of provider. This might be the reason why many find it so difficult to envision, much less *trust*, the unconditional love of God our Father. Many of us are conditioned to view fatherhood as provider first and as nurturing parent a distant second. For countless generations the sign of a "good father" was merely whether he provided food on the table, a roof over the head, and clothes on the back. The father cared solely for the family's financial needs, and their emotional needs were the mother's priority. That vision of fatherhood is a cultural and generational "default" for many, a mind-set that is not easily shaken. The children of Israel held a similar vision, associating their blessings with God's faithfulness and their oppression with a lack of divine love.

What Christ proposed in calling God "Abba" was revolutionary. His invitation to address God as Father required a complete rethinking of previously held and quite sacred concepts. Jesus is **revealing** the Father in terms never before thought possible, the most intimate and interpersonal terms ever uttered about the God of the universe. Jesus Christ **revealed** to us that God's love is measured not merely by the abundance of his generosity (although he is always overly generous) but by the intimacy he offers *every one of his children*, not just his "chosen people."

Christ's **revelation** of Fatherhood, then, has earthly implications as well. All fathers are to mirror the Father's love. Default expectations and preconceived notions regarding fatherhood must disappear. It's as though Jesus is looking at me and saying, "Mark, your fatherhood is not about how many toys you can buy for your children, but about whether you know what your daughters have named each one." This is the intimacy of the heavenly Father I am called to enjoy with my earthly children.

God's fatherhood is eternal; it is his very essence. Christ is the only one who can **reveal** this image of God the Father to us, since he and the Father are one (John 10:30). Consider what it was that made Christ rejoice in St. Luke's Gospel:

In that same hour he [Jesus] rejoiced in the Holy Spirit and said, "I thank you, Father, Lord of heaven and earth, that you have hidden these things from the wise and understanding and **revealed** them to infants; yes, Father, for such was your gracious will. All things have been delivered to me by my Father; and *no one knows who* the Son is except the Father, or who *the Father is except the Son and any one to whom the Son chooses to reveal him.*"

Then turning to the disciples he said privately, "Blessed are the eyes which see what you see! For I tell you that many prophets and kings desired to see what you see, and did not see it, and to hear what you hear, and did not hear it." (Luke 10:21-24; emphasis added)

Those who came before Christ had, in a sense, projected their own ideas of God's Fatherhood onto him, based upon other religions of the time, their own experiences and desires, or their own understanding. No more. Christ came to insure that the people knew the Father as a true Father, not just a God who did fatherly type things. Christ is acknowledging that while others before his earthly arrival may have "known God," *no one until now* knew him as we're going to know him through our newly offered and divine sonship.

Christ offers the same clarity to us. Our own fatherly biases, joys, letdowns, expectations, hopes, fears, and experiences will be **revealed** and healed through the Lord's Prayer. In order to experience the Father who cares *about us*, not just for us, we must invite the Holy Spirit to introduce us more intimately to the Son. Jesus, the Son, will in turn introduce us even more intimately to

God, his (and our) Father. This is what **revelation** is: an unveiling of God by God himself.

We pray the Our Father at every single Mass. Most of you reading this probably pray this prayer every day; I sure do. It's quite easy to fall into the trap of letting that title "Father" be just that, a title for God, rather than the basis for our relationship with him. We could write a long list of traits we look for or expect from a father. Many of our lists would stem from traits we see or desire from our own earthly fathers (again, a projection) rather than from the **revelation** Christ offers us.

### Abba, Father

The phrase "Abba" appears only three times in Sacred Scripture. You should look up these verses and pray through them on your own, as it is well worth your time: Mark 14:36; Romans 8:15; and Galatians 4:6.

Of course, the first time Christ uttered the word "Abba" on this earth, he was likely looking into the eyes of St. Joseph, which is a point that is worthy of mention. God the Father could have chosen to allow the Blessed Virgin to live and work as a single mother. He could have given her a couple of extra guardian angels or sent Elizabeth to care for her. He is the God who created the giraffe, the coffee bean, and cumulus clouds. He does not suffer from a lack of creativity or specificity in his providence, design, or problem solving.

Some suggest that God only had St. Joseph as part of the Holy Family because of cultural expectations, but that is dangerously presumptuous. This is a God who constantly laughs (Psalm 2:4) in the face of social norms. St. Joseph is not window-dressing in the home of the Holy Family; he is nothing less than one of the greatest men to ever walk the planet. A model of manhood and virtue, God *the Father* specifically called and designed Joseph to be the living embodiment of manhood *and fatherhood* to the second Person of the Holy Trinity during his most formative years. In St. Joseph, then, we're given a glimpse into the heart of God the Father. It would be completely illogical to think, after all the trouble of the incarnation, that he would fail to choose a man who reflected his divine image of paternal love with the highest possible measure of human faithfulness.

Scripture **reveals** to us that St. Joseph's love for Mary was outdone *only* by his love for the Father (Matthew 1:19). Only his obedience and belief in the sanctity of the law could lead him to divorce Mary, but his love for her could not allow for harm to come to her, even if he was disgraced in the process. It sounds a lot like the love of God the Father, doesn't it? His vow to the covenant couldn't allow him to just dismiss our sin. "His great love could not allow for him to dismiss us,"[5] even if he was disgraced in the process (Philippians 2:8; Hebrews 12:2).

How heroic the love of God the Father as embodied in Christ's earthly *Abba*, St. Joseph! How many mornings did he rise with the Egyptian sun, an alien in a foreign land, armed only with a tool belt, venturing into a hostile culture seeking enough employment to keep food on the Holy Family's humble dinner table? How disciplined a man to have undoubtedly taught the God of the universe to invoke Scripture each day by praying the sacred *Shema* (the Jewish daily prayers). Echoes of Joseph's and Mary's voices can be heard in Christ's responses to the devil in the wilderness, for his response to the first temptation is quoting the *Shema* he learned at the feet of his parents.

How focused and detail oriented Joseph must have been to make a living as a carpenter, in which the work of your hands points straight back to the craftsmanship of its creator. Could there have been a more perfect metaphor for the earthly father of God? Consider the humility he demonstrated throughout the unique circumstances of Mary's pregnancy. Ponder his obedience in traveling almost one hundred miles with a wife in her third trimester. Contemplate the respect for others' dignity and heritage that Christ undoubtedly learned from his parents (Matthew 2:10-12; John 4:30-42; Matthew 15:24-28). St. Joseph **revealed** the Father to Christ by who he was each day, not merely in what he provided for the family.

## Responding to This Petition

### *Learning what a Father is by knowing what he is not*

Not long after I became a father for the first time, I began journaling more. I cannot recommend this form of prayer highly enough. Journaling reveals a great deal about God and about one's true self. It helped me to reflect on things I've learned about the love of a father since becoming one several years back. The following entry got me to thinking, again, about how a father loves his children. Here are a few "truths" I've learned and realized about good fathers:

- Good fathers aren't afraid of messes—they learn to expect them.

- Good fathers don't like whining—they don't want to listen to it or empower it. They are more inclined to help when children stop whining and speak to them.

- Good fathers know that when things are "too quiet"—when they don't hear their children—they should assume the worst.

- Good fathers usually overdo it with things—they don't just want to provide the minimum; they want to give their kids more than they deserve.

- Good fathers don't base their love on their child's accomplishments. Authentic fatherly love is unconditional.

- Good fathers want their children around—they desire to have their children in their presence as much as possible.

- Good fathers want their children to shine—they rejoice in seeing their children share their gifts and talents with the world.

- Good fathers want to take their child's pain away—they'd rather take it upon themselves.

I strive not merely to be a good father but a great one. I fail daily. I also grow daily, and if, in all of my imperfections, I feel these things for my own kids, how much more does our heavenly Father, all knowing and all perfect in his love (Matthew 7:7-11), feel about us? Consider these "truths" about the Fatherhood that Christ reveals to us:

- My Father in heaven isn't afraid of my messiness. He wants to help me clean it up.

- My Father in heaven doesn't like my whining. He wants me to talk (and listen) to him.

- My Father in heaven knows when I'm sinning, especially when he hasn't heard from me in a while.

- My Father in heaven wants to bless me with more than I truly deserve.

- My Father in heaven loves me unconditionally, not because of what I do, but because I'm his.

- My Father in heaven desires to have me in his presence more often.

- My Father in heaven rejoices when I share my talents (his gifts) with the world.

- My Father in heaven would do anything to take away my pain, even die on a cross.

This is not the fullness of the meaning behind calling God "Abba," but it's a start. How do you, personally, receive and embrace this **revelation** that Christ is imparting to us?

Visit the attic of your heart. Recognize, again, how much your heavenly Father loves you and all that he desires for you (Jeremiah 29:11). Realize, too, that he is listening to your prayers (29:12), and that if you "draw near to God, he will draw near to you" (James 4:8). He is near to you and forever present to you, ready to respond to all your needs.

## Questions for Reflection and Discussion

1. How has your relationship (or lack thereof) with your earthly father influenced your relationship with your heavenly Father? Explain.

2. Consider your life—the good and the bad—and all of your blessings. Name some ways that God the Father has revealed his love to you in how he cares *about* you (parent) and not solely *for* you (provider).

3. What trait do you feel was most important to God that St. Joseph modeled to Jesus as he was growing up? Why?

4. Is it hard for you to believe that God truly loves you for who you are and not for what you do? Why or why not?

# CHAPTER THREE

## "Who Art"

## The Art of **RESPONSE**

**W**e had just returned from a family vacation, one with no laptop, no work calls, and not a single text message sent or received. The word "vacation" comes from the Latin *vacare,* which literally translates "to be unoccupied," which I was. I was unoccupied with anything else in the world that was unrelated to my family or being present to them.

But the minute we returned home, I had to head to the airport for a work trip. My three-year-old daughter entered the room as I was pulling out my bag. "Are you *leaving*, Daddy?" she asked, with tears welling up in her eyes.

I was puzzled at her question, to the point of being almost indignant. Had I not just spent the better portion of five days discussing the intricate ins and outs of various Disney princess story lines? Had I not just packed up every stuffed animal in a six-square-mile radius of our home, transported them across state lines, and followed detailed instructions for their arrangement each night in the hotel bed? Had I not just stopped at every McDonald's restaurant on a ten-hour trip home, one that should have taken less than seven? How could she give me *those eyes?* What more could she possibly want from me? Was she so blind not to see that Daddy now had to leave and actually *make money to pay for the vacation we just enjoyed?* Was she just blind to life's realities?

No, she wasn't. Like Bartimaeus before me, I was the blind one (Mark 10:46).

She had enjoyed my constant and consistent fatherly presence in the previous five days. With the idea of her daddy leaving now, there was a deep void, a true emptiness. I, on the other hand, had made a tactical error in my scheduling plans. I thought that all the time I had been present to my family would leave them wanting less of me, not more. I had properly counted the quantity of time in my schedule but had drastically miscalculated the effects of the quality.

That brings us to these next words of the Lord's Prayer—"who art"—an important reminder and an everlasting promise of the eternal Father's presence. I could be present to my daughter for a few days, but then I had to leave for work. But God can never leave or forsake us (Joshua 1:5). He holds our very existence in his, and he is thinking about us even when we are not thinking about him. We could go for hours without giving God a second thought, but if God failed to think of us for even an instant, we would cease to exist.

Furthermore, while "who art" reminds us of God's constant presence, it also reveals his constant **response** to his children—to our wants, our needs, and our hearts. God is a Father who is always watching, not as a disciplinarian waiting for any misstep, but as the proud father at every sporting event, front row with video camera in hand, refusing to miss a moment of his child's precious life. In our childishness we often want our Father present only when it suits us. How often we desire a Father to respond to our needs without desiring his **response** to our daily life. We want the loan when things are bad, but don't make the phone call when things are good. Our response to God is a lack of presence; God's **response** to us is a constant one.

Our response to our Father "who art"—a Father who is constantly present to us and constantly responding to our needs—is a prayer of gratitude and praise. In this first section of the Lord's Prayer, we are uttering our thanksgiving to God, who is in constant relationship with us, constantly available to us, constantly revealing his love to us, and constantly ready, willing, able, and *waiting* to **respond** to our needs in accordance with his will. This

> **God shows us that true fatherhood is all about sacrifice.**

relationship is far better than having a genie, a butler, or a staff of bodyguards. In this line of the Lord's Prayer, God is promising his constant care, mercy, protection, and love to all *who remain in his love* (John 6:56; 15:4-5). In other words, he is ever present and ever responsive to us, and is hoping we will utilize our free will to be present and responsive to his invitation of love.

For many, it's difficult to envision an ever-present Father of this sort, a father who would sacrifice everything just to be in relationship with us, even his son on a cross. God shows us that true fatherhood is all about sacrifice.

### *Way above par, in a good way*
One Sunday while I was still single, I was at a family gathering, and professional golf was on every available television set. The

commentators were discussing the fact that golfer Phil Mickelson and his wife, Amy, were expecting their first child "at any moment." Apparently, Mickelson had told his caddie, agent, and the golfing officials that if his wife went into labor—even if it happened in the middle of the final championship round—he would leave the course and fly right home. What shocked me, even as a single man without a wife and kids, was the reaction of the fans and the commentators to Phil's decision to leave the tournament if necessary.

"Does he realize what he'd be giving up?" one on-air commentator asked. I thought to myself: "Yes, *he does* understand what he'd be giving up—that's his whole point!"

Phil lost that tournament. In the eyes of many, he lacked focus. He didn't hoist the tournament trophy, but days later, Phil was present for the birth of his child, and I guarantee that heaven applauded.

I recall that tournament often—not the actual match or the drama on the course, but the **response** to Mickelson's bold declaration of priorities. The story was, to me, a micro example of a macro problem. We live in a culture of fatherlessness, as has already been discussed. We also live in a culture that offers little respect or admiration for fathers who have their priorities straight. Cynics veiled as "realists" might say, "Yes, but if he would have won, he could have rolled that paycheck into a savings fund for the child, setting her up for life." I would respond that the child of a father who says, "No way am I going to miss that birth" is far richer than any large check could make her. Fatherhood is more about presence than presents.

*Response-ability*

God, our Father, is love (1 John 4:8). We teach it. We proclaim it. Do we believe it? How often do we really stop to ponder all that those three words contain? Nothing on earth proclaims love the way being present to someone does. My vacation experience drove home this fact to me: Love is spelled t-i-m-e.

## Love is spelled t-i-m-e.

The reading that follows is probably one of the most famous passages in the New Testament. St. Paul wrote it in his first letter to the people of Corinth. You've most likely heard it at weddings. If God is truly love, we should be able to supplant the word "love" with the word "God." I'm going to do just that. I invite you at the end of every sentence to pause and ask yourself, "Do I believe that? Is this my image of God the Father?" Then prayerfully consider your **response** to this radical, revolutionary love.

If I speak in the tongues of men and of angels, but have not **God**, I am a noisy gong or a clanging cymbal. And if I have prophetic powers, and understand all mysteries and all knowledge, and if I have all faith, so as to remove mountains, but have not **God**, I am nothing. If I give away all I have, and if I deliver my body to be burned, but have not **God**, I gain nothing.

**God** is patient and kind; **God** is not jealous or boastful. **God** is not arrogant or rude. **God** does not insist on his own way; **God** is not irritable or resentful; **God** does not rejoice at wrong, but rejoices in the right. **God** bears all things, believes all things, hopes all things, endures all things. **God** never ends. (See 1 Corinthians 13:1-8.)

Dostoevsky once said, "If you love . . . you will perceive the divine mystery in things, and once perceived, you will begin to comprehend it ceaselessly."[6] We need the love of God the Father even to comprehend what true love is and is not. We need the Trinity to see perfect love in action—a relationship that requires a **response** from the other Person.

So we either accept God's love or we reject God's love. Some might say, "I do neither; I'm indifferent." That indifference, at its

> ## God gives us free will, and with that free will an ability to accept or reject his love.

root, is a rejection, just a slow and painfully indecisive one. If my wife stood at the altar pledging her love and saying "I do," and I shrugged her off, unwilling to **respond**, that lack of response is, indeed, a response (one that would have killed her after she had killed me!). God gives each of us free will, and with that free will, an ability to accept or reject his love. In fact, at every minute of the day, we are being faced with choices that will either draw us closer to the love of God or lead us away from his enduring love (see Deuteronomy 30:15-19).

Many in the modern age fear that God the "Father" either spun creation into existence and then abandoned it completely, or that he is very much alive but completely divorced from us and uncaring about what happens to us. Either scenario leaves us very timid in our **response** to "our Father who art." Our fear that God is not *unconditionally* loving or *eternally* present leaves us apprehensive about responding to his invitation of love. We fear that he suffers from the same human frailties, limitations, or selfishness that we've seen in so many earthly fathers. As a result, many of us are unwilling to **respond** for fear of getting hurt or being let down, once again. We want him to prove his love, again and again, before we put ourselves "out there," so to speak. The incarnation, the passion, the crucifixion, the resurrection, the ascension, the institution of the Church: What else do we need to open our hearts to his?

## Leaving the ninety-nine

I'm a logical man. I appreciate order. I like when things add up and make sense. In this way, God and his lack of (what I consider to be) logic drive me absolutely crazy. His decisions don't make sense to me; his methods confuse me. For example, Aaron was a priest and obviously a capable communicator. Why didn't God go to Aaron in the first place? No, he wanted Moses, the stuttering murderer, hiding out in the wilderness (see Exodus 4). What about Stephen? He was one of the original deacons, so filled with passion and love for the Lord that he was willing to give up his very life. Why didn't God have Stephen become his great missionary to the world? No, he wanted Saul (Paul), the man who stood there watching as Stephen was stoned to death (see Acts 7:55–8:1). God warned me about this part of his nature through the prophet Isaiah:

> For my thoughts are not your thoughts, / neither are your ways my ways, says the LORD. / For as the heavens are higher than the earth, / so are my ways higher than your ways / and

my thoughts than your thoughts. (Isaiah 55:8-9)

Then Christ poses the question about the ninety-nine sheep:

"What man of you, having a hundred sheep, if he has lost one of them, does not leave the ninety-nine in the wilderness, and go after the one which is lost, until he finds it?" (Luke 15:4)

My response would be "I don't; I let one go to save the ninety-nine." Thank God I'm not God, right? His **response** to our sin is to offer us the gift of salvation through the cross, the sacraments, and the Church. The **response** of our Father in heaven is that he cannot leave us on our own, mired in our own iniquities and transgressions. The **response** of God is the **response** of perfect love: He is going to offer us salvation, even when we fail to accept it. His love is illogical to us because it is perfect. We are so accustomed to counterfeit forms of love that when authentic love stands before us—and chases after us even when we're the ones who have gone astray—we doubt its sincerity.

Logic gets in the way of my loving well. Intimacy, true intimacy, isn't about logic; it's about total presence and self-gift. Love is a gift, a gift that demands a **response**. Oftentimes we respond in a way that makes sense for us rather than in a way that puts the other first. God doesn't demand that we love him. He invites us to love him because he knows something that we often forget: His love is perfect and unfailing. God's love is not fickle, and his presence is not temporary. God's love and presence are eternal; that's what we are celebrating when we pray "who art." Our **response** to the God who is eternally present to us should be to do everything in our power to be more present to him. That's the only **response** worthy of his love: We must be present to his presence.

## Responding to This Petition

### *A holy hour makes us holier*

As Catholics, the greatest reminder we have of God's eternal presence is the Eucharist, which is on every altar and in every tabernacle on earth. The word "tabernacle" literally means "tent." God the Father so desires to be present *with us and to us* that he has literally pitched his tent in every conceivable corner of the world—in every country, region, and culture—to insure his availability and accessibility to us. How is that for presence? How is that for an everlasting **response** to our need for a Father? How is that for a dad who will never abandon us—not physically, not emotionally, not spiritually—but who is available to us at any hour of the day?

Are you willing to be present to him—for an hour a week, perhaps? Does your parish have perpetual adoration of the Blessed Sacrament? If not, how about finding a time when you can hold vigil in the church, just you and the Lord? Are you willing to respond to his invitation?

Our Father "who art" could not **respond** to our needs any more if he tried. The candle that burns beside his dwelling place is the constant reminder of his daily **response**, veiled as common bread, to all those walking in darkness. His light beckons us to the altar table and, ultimately, into his arms in heaven.

## Questions for Reflection and Discussion

1. What are God's constant presence and faithfulness to us supposed to teach us? How can we be more like God in this way? Give practical examples.

2. What would need to change in your daily or weekly schedule for you to become more present to God speaking to you and loving you?

3. What is the difference between physical presence and emotional presence, in your opinion? Do you see that difference in yourself or in others at Mass?

4. Would you characterize your relationship with God as intimate? On a scale of one to ten (being the highest), how intimate is your relationship with God the Father? Explain.

5. If you frequently attend adoration of the Blessed Sacrament, what are some of the words or expressions you would use to describe how it leaves you feeling? If you don't pray in adoration frequently (or have never gone), is there something specific that keeps you from it? Discuss.

# CHAPTER FOUR

# "In Heaven"

# The Journey toward Our **REUNION**

Every ten years an adult is offered the opportunity for self-evaluation and growth. This event, for some, creates more anxiety than any birthday and more stress than any project at work. It's the high school reunion.

Movies and television shows portray reunions with a host of clichés: a high school gym decorated with streamers, the varsity football heroes still wearing their lettermen jackets, the cheerleaders still gossiping. And there is the mandatory story line of the geek who is now a millionaire. With this in mind, I was relieved and pleased that my ten-year high school reunion was nothing of the sort. No, there was just a big room filled with various strangers and a good deal of liquor-masked discomfort. Conversations revealed a variety of things, but consistently only two themes really caught my attention.

First, many of the people I encountered were trapped in the past. Every story they shared was from ten years ago. They so longed to live in their glory days of high school that when the conversation was moved to the present, it was quickly guided back to a time when they were thinner, younger, more popular, or free of responsibility. I left confident that if there had been a time machine available, it would have drawn a longer line than the one for the ladies' restroom.

Second, I noticed a large number of people who in no way wanted to talk about the past; high school was, for them, very thankfully over. Interestingly, however, many of these people didn't want to talk about the present either. They would offer a little information about their spouses or kids or jobs. But most of the conversation was spent talking about their plans for the future: their next trip, their next purchase, their next achievement, their next step into greater professional waters. I heard more about their eventual dream home than I did about their current one, more about where their kids would go to college than where they were going to elementary school.

There were some people who talked about the present, but they were in the minority. When I reflected on the night, it struck me how difficult it can be for many in our culture, myself included, to really be present to the present. Some of us are trapped in the past—or in past sins. Some are consumed with the future—or with anxiety and worry about the uncontrollable. But God calls us to live in the present, to trust the past to his mercy (Isaiah 1:18) and the future to his providence (Matthew 6:34).

One of the greatest challenges in Christianity is to live for the future while still being in the present. Being present to God takes prayer, a lot of prayer. Prayer can't just come off the shelf on Sundays, holidays, or when Grandma is diagnosed cancer. No, prayer has to begin and end our day. Prayer ultimately leads us to heaven because it constantly keeps us focused on our God. And if he is our ultimate goal, then we are headed for a **reunion** of grandiose proportions with him in heaven. St. Paul spoke of this yearning for a heavenly **reunion** with God:

Forgetting what lies behind and straining forward to what lies ahead, I press on toward the goal for the prize of the upward call of God in Christ Jesus. . . . Our commonwealth *is in heaven,* and from it we await a Savior, the Lord Jesus Christ, who will change our lowly body to be like his glorious body. (Philippians 3:13-14, 20-21; emphasis added)

St. Paul was reminding the Philippians (and us) that keeping our eyes fixed on our **reunion** with God in heaven does not mean that we live in the future. Rather, we must pay attention to

## How do we focus on living for heaven without losing this moment of our faith journey?

the consequences of our actions and decisions in the present. We "strain" and "press on toward the goal" when we unleash God's grace within us *now*, in the present moment. Living in God's grace demands that we allow ourselves neither to get trapped in the past by sins nor suffocated by the future in our desire to control. We need to be **reunited** with God every moment of the day in prayer (1 Thessalonians 5:17), and in doing so, we will enjoy that **reunion** with our Father in heaven every time we call upon him until he calls us home.

So what is it that gets in our way of this joyful **reunion**? What traps us in the past or consumes us with the future? How do we focus on living for heaven without losing this moment of our faith journey? Ask yourself right now: Has *today* thus far reflected a desire for heaven or earth? Sometimes our desire to be seen as "something" in the eyes of the world interferes with our desire for Someone in heaven.

### The right and the left

The apostles often failed to grasp the totality or depth of the truths that Jesus lived and taught. Such was the case in this gospel episode involving an exchange between Jesus and the sons of Zebedee. The apostles had heard Jesus' warnings about earthly possessions and about the dangers of having the wrong perspective on wealth. Perhaps James and John, two of Jesus' closest followers, thought that being part of the "inner circle" should make them eligible for something even more glamorous.

> And James and John, the sons of Zebedee, came forward to him, and said to him, "Teacher, we want you to do for us whatever we ask of you." And he said to them, "What do you want me to do for you?" And they said to him, "Grant us to sit, one at your right hand and one at your left, in your glory." But Jesus said to them, "You do not know what you are asking. Are you able to drink the chalice that I drink, or to be baptized with the baptism with which I am baptized?" And they said to him, "We are able." And Jesus said to them, "The chalice that I drink you will drink; and with the baptism with which I am baptized, you will be baptized; but to sit at my right hand or at my left is not mine to grant, but it is for those for whom it has been prepared. (Mark 10:35-40)

The brothers' desire was not only to be included in the royal court as the new kingdom was ushered in but to be sitting in seats of power, clothed in esteem and worldly recognition. Their goal was not just to be on Jesus' VIP list but to be the bouncers, throwing out those who didn't belong at the party. *They sought to be on Christ's right and left* as he came into the kingdom. The next time we see these words in St. Mark's Gospel is in chapter 15:

> And with him they crucified two robbers, *one on his right* and *one on his left.* (Mark 15:27; emphasis added)

The cup that James and John were so quick to confirm that they'd drink was the cup of suffering that Christ himself was dreading—to the point of sweating his own blood—in the Garden of Gethsemane. When Jesus came into his glory, the ones on his right and left were dying too. The tutorial that the sons of Zebedee received on the road that day was one that they would not forget. How quickly do we forget it? How quickly do we seek the gold of earth, forgetting that gold is mere pavement in heaven (see Revelation 21:21)?

**Our salvation may cost us nothing, but true discipleship costs us everything.**

What does being in Christ's "royal court" get you on earth? It offers you incredible joy, healthy relationships, spiritual freedom, life purpose, unconditional forgiveness, and eternal love. It also offers a point to your suffering. That's right, as good as it is—and it is good, *very good* to walk with Christ—it's also a walk beset with sufferings. The royal court extends the invitation to an abundant life, but it also carries with it hardship. Our salvation may cost us nothing, but true discipleship costs us everything. That's how the servant becomes the greatest (Mark 10:43)—by dying to the old self and rising to the new creation, on a road paved with temporary suffering but eternal bliss.

### *What no one would wish*

Homework is a dreaded word in the Hart home. For my kids, it's a task to complete. For my wife and me, it's an opportunity to grow—our kids grow in wisdom, and we grow in patience. Virtue abounds . . . sometimes. The problem is that my daughter's goal is not my goal. She wants to get it over with; I want her to get something out of it. Her annoyance grows in proportion to my obstinacy. I refuse to let her cut corners because of my love for her, now and later. She views homework as a time of suffering, but I view it as a time of growth. We have different goals.

The same is true of our outlook on life. Life is often filled with suffering when our goal and God's goal are different. God's goal for us is to be in perfect communion with him, a **reunion**

> **Life is often filled with suffering when our goal and God's goal are different.**

in heaven. Our goal is to not suffer here on earth. On most days our desire to avoid suffering outweighs our desire for an existence without suffering in heaven tomorrow. We seek to avoid suffering at all costs, and logically so. Wisdom tells us, though, that it is through suffering, not through comfort, that we mature. It's through suffering that we grow closest to Christ (see Romans 5:3; 2 Corinthians 1:5; Philippians 3:10; Colossians 1:24).

Our earthly goal is to avoid suffering. Some suffering is a result of our own sin and is unnecessary. Other suffering comes in the form of trials that God allows to grow us in virtue (see James 1:2; 1 Peter 4:3; Romans 5:4). Christ's passion reminds us that the path to heaven is strewn with rocks and the crown of righteousness is woven from thorns. That is one reason why we as Catholics embrace a splintered crucifix rather than a shiny cross. There is no Easter Sunday without Good Friday; if you want to live, you must first learn how to die (see Luke 9:23-24).

If we trust God our Father and believe that his ultimate goal for us is that heavenly **reunion,** we will stay on the straight and very narrow path that so many others avoid (Matthew 7:13-14). The path to God might be long and winding, rocky and steep, but it's on that road that he travels to meet us in **reunion.**

### *Reunion on a road*

See if you recognize the following three verses. They come from the most famous parable in Scripture.

> "I will arise and go to my father, and I will say to him, 'Father, I have sinned against heaven and before you; I am no longer worthy to be called your son; treat me as one of your hired servants.'" And he arose and came to his father. But while he was yet at a distance, his father saw him and had compassion, and ran and embraced him and kissed him. (Luke 15:18-20)

This passage from St. Luke comes to us from the famous parable of the prodigal son. You, like me, have probably heard the story hundreds of times, but often it's with the stories we've heard the most frequently that we miss some of the most important details.

Because of the outcome of this story, people have often believed the term prodigal to be a good thing. Well, it is and it isn't. The word actually means "recklessly wasteful," as in the case of the son—who had foolishly spent his entire inheritance on the temporary and the worldly. The word "prodigal" also means "extremely generous," however, as in the case of the father, who was amazingly generous with his mercy, compassion, and fortune to his returning son. One of the most impressive parts of this story, though, is contained in verse 20. It says that he *ran* to his son.

Now, keep in mind that the son had asked for his inheritance before the father was even dead; in that culture, doing so was a huge slap in the face and a sign of great disrespect. Not only had the son quickly spent all the money, but he had wasted it on "loose living" (Luke 15:13). It had gotten so bad that he was, literally, lying in the mud and fighting the pigs for food. And now, looking at the mess his life had become—professionally, socially, and literally—he decided to return to his father and beg his forgiveness.

Here is where the story changes. It goes from being the story of a prodigal son who wasted his undeserved blessings to one about the prodigal father, who seems to waste (in the eyes of the older brother) his mercy and forgiveness on a child who wished him dead and deserted the family.

We're shown, though, that the mercy was not a waste, not in the eyes of the father.

Upon seeing his son returning, the father *could have* sat in the house, waiting for the son. He could have sat on the porch, refusing to forgive his son upon his approach. The father could have made the son publicly grovel at his feet. He could have put him to work as a hired hand or slave. Instead, the father not only forgave him but ran to meet him. Incidentally, in that culture, a man of the father's age and stature who went "running" was considered incredibly undignified. It was inappropriate, and it wasn't done.

> **Mercy was not a waste, not in the eyes of the father.**

When they were finally face-to-face, the father did not condemn the child for the mess he had made of his life. He did not wait for him to get rid of his filthy clothes or swine-like smell. No, the Father embraced the returning and repentant son because that is what parents do—they love, even when the children haven't acted in such a way as to deserve it.

In a similar way, even when I make a mess of my life—through selfishness, poor decisions, or apathy—God waits to embrace me in my messiness. God isn't waiting for me to pursue him. His eyes are scanning the horizon, looking for me to return and hoping at each moment that I will. God is pursuing me, ready to run to me and meet me on the road for a **reunion** that will make the angels sing. Even if I feel that I'm too messy, or that he is wasting his time or mercy on me, he loves me all the more, and loves me *prodigally*, with extreme and unlimited generosity.

## Responding to This Petition

### *Reunions offered daily*

Earthly esteem and riches mean nothing to God. They are nothing compared to the kingdom of heaven that awaits us (1 Corinthians 2:9). In fact, we don't even have to wait for death to experience a foretaste of this **reunion** with the Father. Where Christ went, the kingdom of heaven went with him. Where Christ is, heaven is within reach. Every time we go to Mass, heaven is stooping down to greet us and lift us up to a new consciousness. At every Mass we are **reunited** with our Father in heaven (see *Catechism of the Catholic Church*, 1090).

When was the last time you attended daily Mass? It may seem like a challenge. It may appear to you like an extra "burden" in your schedule. But what is worth having that doesn't necessitate some sacrifice? How different our lives would look if we set up our days and weeks around daily Mass! While it's not always possible due to varying Mass times and work schedules, it can often be achieved at least once or twice a week, if we're willing to be creative.

Why are there so few people at daily Masses? Is it only the inflexibility of the workday or the inconvenience of the Mass times, or is it more? Is it that we don't really hunger for the Eucharist because we have doubts about its being the Real Presence? If so, it's time to study our faith and pray about those doubts. Is it because we "don't get much out of Mass," and it's not engaging us enough to reorganize the workweek around? If so, again, it's time to study our faith and pray about those feelings. Is it because there just aren't enough hours in the day? If so, it may be time to take a hard look at our schedules, discerning what can be eliminated from our overbooked week to make room in our lives for God. Keep feeding your faith with the Eucharist, and trust that eventually, all of your doubts will starve to death.

As we see here, it is never a "waste" to run to God; it's a waste of time not to run to him. He's calling our name, and he loves us enough to allow us to call him by his.

## Questions for Reflection and Discussion

1. What percentages of your prayer are directed toward the past, the present, and the future?

2. Is heaven something that weighs into your daily decisions on a regular basis? When does it enter your mind? Explain.

3. As was discussed, God allows some suffering as trials to help us grow. Name a time of suffering that, looking back, you can see was actually a time in which you grew in God's love.

4. If you were to die today, what would the Father say to you when your eyes met? Is there anything more you need to do or say or change on earth before this reunion?

5. How do you view Mass? Is it more as an encounter with God or as an obligation?

# CHAPTER FIVE

# "Hallowed Be Thy Name"
# The Invitation to **REVERENCE**

There are many conversations a husband and wife have when they find out they are expecting a child. Some have to do with impending changes to the home or the financial situation. Many surround the logistics of raising children, including work schedules, day care, or the need to be closer to (or farther from) family. One conversation that certainly has the propensity to bring a couple closer or to drive a wedge is deciding on the new baby's name.

For each generation, certain names are popular. Some names go in and out of style; others seem to effortlessly stand the test of time. Many Catholics desire the name of a saint or Bible hero, which is what my own mother did for me and for which I am now grateful. Although I did not grow up fond of my name, I have since grown in great admiration for St. Mark and St. Joseph (my middle name)—they have become two of my daily intercessors and heroes.

No matter what criteria are used to select a baby's name, there's no doubt that names are important. They communicate a great deal about us. Names convey not only who we are but also, in many cases, *how we would like to be known*. Consider how people introduce themselves. Do they go by their birth name or, perhaps, by a nickname or common abbreviation? Actors often change their names to make themselves more marketable. Few would have turned out for a western starring Marion Morrison; millions turned out to see Morrison as John Wayne.

Sometimes a courtship begins when a man walks over to meet a woman he finds attractive and asks for her name. When he asks for that name, he is certainly seeking much more: The name is a

> ## There's more to the name than just the name.

small gift of oneself. It is at once an invitation into the woman's world while also an affirmation of the fellow's manhood. When the man gets "the name and number," it's the first step toward a relationship and toward greater intimacy—perhaps even marriage.

There's more to the name than just the name.

### *What's in a name?*

When Moses left his herd, he was also looking at a beautiful—and very unusual—sight: an "angel of the LORD appeared to him in a flame of fire out of the midst of a bush." When he looked more closely, he realized that the bush "was burning, yet it was not consumed" (Exodus 3:2). It's in this encounter that Moses' (and our) relationship with God is forever changed. God had a mission for Moses; Moses had a question for God. During this theophany, Moses did something unprecedented: He asked God for his name. It was an irreverent question for the shoeless shepherd to ask (3:5), but one that would ultimately lead to great **reverence**.

The request sounds simple enough. If Moses is to deliver God's message to a nation of enslaved peers and to Pharaoh, the most powerful man on the planet, it seems logical that he would want to know the name of him for whom he is speaking.

> Then Moses said to God, "If I come to the sons of Israel and say to them, 'The God of your fathers has sent me to you,' and they ask me, 'What is his name?' what shall I say to them?" God said to Moses, "I AM WHO I AM." (Exodus 3:13-14)

Beyond the ethereal ramifications of the timeless, all-powerful God of the universe sharing an intimate conversation with a humble shepherd in the Midian desert 3,600 years ago, this exchange doesn't strike us as that odd. In the Mediterranean world, however, the request and revelation of a name was not something to be taken lightly.

Earlier in Genesis, we're given a small glimpse into the profundity of this occurrence when Isaac's son, Jacob, finds himself in a late-night wrestling match with an angel (Genesis 32:22-30). Jacob and the angel of God are embroiled in a long battle. As the dawn breaks and there is no clear victor, Jacob—realizing that he has faced no mere mortal—asks his competitor for a blessing. Prior to blessing Jacob, however, the angel asks his name, and then promptly changes it to *Israel* (which means "one who contends with God"). The offering of the name, though, is the overlooked portion of the story. "The yielding of the name was an act of submission. When Jacob surrendered his name, he surrendered his soul. He relinquished authority over his own life.

With the surrender came a new name, a new identity, *Israel*."[7] The changing of the name signified the changing of Jacob's essence.

We fast-forward several hundred years now, back to Moses. Moses was asking for the name, not because he wanted God to submit to him, but because he wanted to know the God to whom he was submitting himself. God's willingness to share his holy name with us is incredible in what it signifies. Our knowing of God's name signifies something even more: an invitation into a relationship and a new accessibility with the God of the universe. Knowing God's name is an invitation to call upon him, to walk with him, to know him. As Dr. Scott Hahn puts it, "The name of God is consecrated. It is holy. God's name is not merely transcendent and mysterious; it is intimate and personal and interpersonal."[8]

This exchange of names was not an exchange of identification by which God could flex his divine muscles in the face of the Egyptian gods (they would be exposed as false throughout the ten plagues—see Exodus 7–12). The giving of his name was the beginning of a new covenant with his people, a new courtship by which God would try to "woo" their hearts once again. And as Exodus unfolds, we read about the plagues, the Passover, the daring escape through the Red Sea, and the journey to Mount Sinai. During this journey of faith, the children of God have a new access to the God of creation; this access comes precisely through his sacred name.

Since covenants had been broken, however, this new covenant through Moses was going to carry some parameters with it for our own good. God had put himself "out there," so to speak, in giving us his holy name. He had humbled himself and made himself vulnerable, for once the holy name is known, it can be misused.

With the gift of the name, which calls for **reverence**, comes the threat of irreverence in words and ways.

### Thou shalt not use my name in traffic!

Prior to the Vegas-like encounter that Moses had with a bush, people in the Book of Genesis knew God by various "names." When Abraham, Isaac, Jacob, or Joseph spoke of God, it was by a designation, a title attributed to him because of some great work he had wrought with his own hands or an oath he had made with his own voice.

Those early names were titles that had more to do with what God "does" than with who he is; they identified him by his works and deeds more than by his true essence, which is love (1 John 4:8). When Moses was entrusted with God's name, it was an affirmation of his own worth, which comes from God, because God had never before bestowed such an honor on a per-

## God trusted Moses' motivations in asking for and invoking his holy name.

son. Although Moses had a "past"—he had murdered a man in Egypt (see Exodus 2:11-12)—God knew his heart and recognized him as a meek and humble man (Numbers 12:3). God trusted Moses' motivations in asking for and invoking his holy name. He knows our motivations too. Are they always as pure when *we* invoke God's name?

God's name, revealed to Moses as JHVH or YHWH, translates to "I AM" and is known as the sacred tetragrammaton (from a Greek word meaning "four letters"). The name is articulated as either "Jehovah" or "Yahweh," yet it was not to be spoken aloud. This holy name is a holy designation of the inestimable God of the universe. To invoke the name was to claim to be equal to him. Calling on God for aid or in praise and adoration was acceptable, but invoking God's unutterable name was blasphemy. Over the centuries the restrictions in regard to uttering the name have become more relaxed.

In 2008, however, Pope Benedict XVI issued a reminder to liturgists and musicians that even music used within the Mass (hymns such as "Yahweh, I Know You Are Near") ought to be rethought so as to maintain a holy **reverence** for the unutterable name of the almighty Father. The pope's proclamation was not intended to be a rebuke but an invitation to constantly discern how **reverently** we do or do not invoke the name of God. The Holy Father echoes what Christ reminds us of in the gospels. It's not what comes out of our mouths that makes us holy, but what comes out of our hearts (Matthew 15:11). God desires our holiness (1 Thessalonians 4:7).

To be holy means to be "consecrated" or "set apart" for a reason. We set things apart and revere them in an effort to keep them special, to maintain a level of purity. It is through an awareness of sacredness, an awareness of holiness, that we are invited into **reverence**.

### Isn't anything sacred anymore?

**Reverence** comes from the Latin *reverentia,* meaning "to stand in awe of." Reverence goes well beyond our speech. It has to do with our entire being, our posture, inside and out. Our **reverence** for the holy name of God, for example, should be reflected not only in our speech but also in the heart that motivates the speech, the mind that processes it, and the will that controls it.

So what do we **revere** in our modern culture? Oh, so many things.

We revere fame. We revere fortune. We revere status. We revere the logo on the car and the brand of the jeans. We revere the designer of the shoes and the maker of the sunglasses. We revere the artist and the athlete, the money man and the musician.

Consider that pornography is the highest-grossing industry in America by far, eclipsing the gross revenues of all professional sports and major television networks. The highest-grossing movies amongst American teenagers over the past several years have been "slasher" horror films, followed by sex "comedies" as a close second. Music has become more profane and suggestive. Video games are increasingly violent and graphic. Divorce rates climb. Demands for gay marriage continue to grow in intensity. Well over forty-five million babies have been legally killed since 1973.

We've lost our way. We've lost our **reverence**. It's not that *everything* has to be sacred in this secular culture, it's that *some things* ought to remain sacred. Marriage needs to be seen as a sacred commitment (Matthew 19:6). The human body needs to be revered as a sacred body (1 Corinthians 6:19), not merely the means to a pornographic end. The womb needs to be revered as a place of life again, not a tomb for the unborn. In short, the minute we stop revering our Creator, all that is made in the image and likeness (Genesis 1:26-17) of that Creator is ripe for irreverence.

As Catholics, we need to look inward and see what we hold sacred and revere. Sacred Scripture and Tradition demand our reverence, as do sacred silence and sacred spaces. The sacraments (literally "sacred oaths" or "sacred mysteries") need to be revered, in particular the sacraments of vocation: holy matrimony and holy orders.

> **As Catholics, we need to look inward and see what we hold sacred and revere.**

The priesthood used to be revered—and still is by many. However, since the pedophilia scandal, priests in many dioceses feel they must continually prove themselves to earn the respect of the masses. Holy days used to be revered. Originally they were seen as opportunities to rejoice, to celebrate the great things that God had done (and continues to do) throughout salvation history. Sadly, they're now often seen as archaic, and these special days, hallowed and set apart for good reason, are viewed through a lens of inconvenience and irrelevance.

## Responding to This Petition

### *The importance of the family name*

In the "great commissioning," our Lord gives us an invaluable insight into God's name, which is our own family name. He tells us:

> "Go therefore and make disciples of all nations, baptizing them in the name of the Father and of the Son and of the Holy Spirit, teaching them to observe all that I have

commanded you; and behold, I am with you always, to the close of the age." (Matthew 28:19-20)

A closer examination of this passage in Greek shows us that it's not merely "in the name" (formulaic) but "*into* the name" (familial). Now, that might strike us as a minor difference, but it has major ramifications and implications.

When Christ commissioned his apostles to baptize people *into the name*, he may as well have said "into the family"—the family of the Blessed Trinity. "In the name of the Father and of the Son and of the Holy Spirit" is more than the words said at the Sacrament of Baptism or for the Sign of the Cross. It is a call to bring people into the family, a divine family of perfect love. When the man offers the cliché "Hey, what's your sign?" to a Christian woman, the best response would be "the sign of the cross," for it is in the cross that we find our identity, our family name, and our true heritage.

Why would God desire us to be brought up into this holy name, his family of perfect love? God's family is holy and sacred. God's name stands out—or ought to stand out—in a world in which there is often little that is holy or sacred. What *and who* we **revere** says as much about us as what and who we do not. If we are open to standing up—and thus standing out—in a culture of irreverence, refusing to profane the family name, as so many others do in speech or in conduct, we will assuredly be mocked too. If we are truly part of God's family, though, we will understand that someone defaming his name is the same as someone defaming *our name*, because we are baptized *into his name*. God's name is our name.

Imagine standing in the throne room of God, surrounded by his glory, blinded by his perfection, heart rent and knees bent. How would you address him? Would your voice quiver? Would your hands shake? Would your heart race and your mouth dry out? Would you mindlessly profane his name in casual conversation to make a point, as so many do on earth? Would you feel free to use his holy name—the name above every other name (Philippians 2:9-10)—in any other way than in worship? No, of course you wouldn't. No sane person would do such a thing. We are to hallow God's name, to *revere* it, "on earth as it is in heaven" (but we'll deal more with that in chapter eight).

His name is to be our name. His kingdom is designed to be our kingdom.

## Questions for Reflection and Discussion

1. Why did your parents name you the name that they did? What was their reasoning or rationale? Additionally, if you are confirmed, why did you choose the confirmation saint's name that you did?

2. Do you ever struggle with taking the Lord's name in vain? In what environment (school, work, home, the media, etc.) do you hear this commandment toward reverence broken the most? What effect does it have on the holiness of that environment?

3. What makes your home a reverent home? What have you done or could you do to insure that it is a sacred place?

4. How can the sacraments of vocation (matrimony and holy orders) be revered again in this culture? What can you personally do to encourage a reverence for these sacraments and vocations?

*CHAPTER SIX*

# "Thy Kingdom Come"
## The Challenge of **RENOUNCEMENT**

**N**othing could have prepared me for childbirth, nothing in the world. Pregnancy classes discuss practical skills. Other dads share life lessons and whatever wisdom they've drawn from personal failures. Books are written, blogs published, and jokes made, but when the time comes to head into that delivery room, you're on your own. Life is happening all around you, and right before your bloodshot eyes you are given a choice: interact with it or get out of the way.

There I was in the delivery room. I was ready. I had the breathing down. I held my wife's hand in my right hand, my rosary in my left. I was prepared. The camera battery was charged. I had contacted every priest in my speed dial. After the blessedly safe delivery of my first daughter, my amateur photo shoot began. Within minutes I had a hundred pictures and live video footage. Within an hour I had e-mailed pictures to everyone in my address book. As they cleaned up my new miracle and my wife dozed off for a well-earned nap, I sat bedside with a new Web page announcing her birth already near completion. I don't mind saying it: I was the Father of the Year.

Joyful (and prideful), I reclined in my chair for the last few moments of silence I'd enjoy for the next eighteen years or so.

As a lover of Sacred Scripture, I then did something I rarely do. I played "Bible Bingo" (in which you open to a randomly selected page to "see what God has to say to you"). I opened up to chapter two of the Gospel of Matthew, which read:

> Now when Jesus was born in Bethlehem of Judea in the days of Herod the king, behold, Wise Men from the East came to Jerusalem, saying, "Where is he who has been born king of the Jews? For we have seen his star in the East, and have come to worship him." (Matthew 2:1-2)

Then it hit my like the proverbial bolt of lightning right between the eyes: God does things with style. And here he was giving me a dose of humility. I learned some breathing, took some pictures, made some announcements, and started a Web page. God made a star.

God made a star to announce his proudest father moment. He propelled a flaming orb high into his heavens to guide gentile astronomers thousands of miles with gifts fit for a king. I bought an overpriced teddy bear from a hospital gift shop.

When God's kingdom came to earth—in the flesh—he made it known. Everyone from that moment on in history would be given a chance to encounter God in a new and incredible way. They would have an incredible choice to **renounce** their vision and version of an earthly kingdom in favor of one that would never fade.

My fatherhood included a **renouncement** of my former way of life. Fatherhood joyfully strips you of selfishness and self-centeredness with every passing day. Every moment of fatherhood carries with it the opportunity to **renounce** my worldly desires in favor of

God's heavenly-laid plans. Again, parenthood shows God's great style. He not only allows his creation to participate in the very act of creation with him but he blesses control freaks (like me) out of control in the process. He shakes us free of worldly, created things as he entrusts a young soul to us that is uncreated by us.

God builds his kingdom by bringing more pure souls (babies) into his kingdom, all the while entrusting the care and catechesis

## God is creative. God has style.

of these souls to older, imperfect souls (us) that he blesses out of their own self-reliance. God is creative. God has style even in the way he invites us to sacrifice our own "kingdoms" and to build his kingdom rather than our own.

### His kingdom has come

When Jesus Christ spoke of the kingdom of God, he was not speaking merely of heaven or of judgment day. When Christ came, the kingdom of God came with him. For three very public years, that "kingdom" touched lepers, forgave adulterers, ate with tax collectors, and scandalized the pompous and prideful establishment of his day. And since the kingdom goes where he goes, we experience a taste of the kingdom when we encounter our Eucharistic Lord who is still with us (Matthew 28:20; 1 Corinthians 11:23-29). His kingdom is encountered in every imaginable corner of the earth, in every known language, whether legal or illegal, supported or suppressed, through rituals or relationships. His kingdom is here, and it is thriving. Bethlehem is as close as your parish tabernacle. The River Jordan flows from every sanctuary. Calvary is as near as your church's altar.

God's kingdom has come. It is here; it's just not fully manifest. It hasn't come to full fruition yet. That will take time—the end of time, to be precise. Our parishes are the living nativity sets of life. The Eucharistic altar table is the first manger all over again. The kingdom of God is before us and around us. We just need eyes to see it. Clarity of vision does not come easily in a culture in which vision is so often and so freely blurred. Before we can announce "thy kingdom" that has come, we need to **renounce** my kingdom that has been—that has been existent in its pitiful lack of glory. Put simply, "Thy kingdom come" means "My kingdom go."

### *I have a renouncement to make*

Several years ago I gave away everything I owned. I mean that literally—I got rid of *everything*. I don't say this to boast. I'd love to say that it was a decision I was led to through deep prayer, but that wouldn't be entirely accurate. I'd love to claim that I had read the life of St. Francis of Assisi and in a moment of humble surrender was inspired to leave it all behind and follow Christ (Matthew 4:20; Luke 9:60). That would be an outright lie. The reason that I gave away everything I owned? I got married. The fact that I received no money for any of my worldly possessions should tell you something about the bacteria-ridden bachelor pad I was living in and the state of my "furniture" (please note the quotes). I was left with only the shirt on my back. Even my clothes were given away. My wife loved me and, in that love, could not let me go out in public so oblivious to style any longer.

I'll admit that I had a little separation anxiety at first, but I quickly grew thankful for my wife and, more to the point, for the Sacrament of Holy Matrimony. The sacraments of the Catholic Church are tremendous gifts of God's grace. The sacraments offer us an encounter with Christ himself. The *Catechism of the Catholic Church* is a tremendous source of wisdom on the sacraments and worth a slow reading (see 1210–1666).

From my experience, in a definition you won't read in the *Catechism*, I'd offer this: The sacraments are designed to destroy you. That's right, the sacraments are designed to destroy *you* and leave only God within you. We call this life of God within us grace. Consider baptism, when death is put to death. Consider reconciliation, when sin is transformed into grace. Consider matrimony or holy orders, in which our selfishness is tested at every turn, in which every day we have the opportunity to die to ourselves so that others will see, know, and experience the unconditional love of God the Father. The sacraments fulfill the words of St. Paul, who knew that it was "no longer I who live, but Christ who lives in me" (Galatians 2:20).

> **I had to renounce all of those worldly and earthly things that promised me security and happiness apart from God.**

The veil that was lifted through my sacrament was not made of lace; it was a veil of lies. I had to **renounce** all of those worldly and earthly things that promised me security and happiness apart from God. My kingdom had been stripped away, and as difficult as it is at times, truthfully, I couldn't be happier about it. Whose kingdom are *you* beseeching when you pray the Lord's Prayer?

When we **renounce** the things of creation that we allow to bind us, we are more perfectly bound to the Creator (2 Corinthians 5:15). **Renouncement** is the key to living out this petition of "Thy kingdom come." Renouncement is how we move from "my" to "thy." Renouncement is how our miniature and individual kingdom pursuits give way to one, holy, catholic, and apostolic kingdom of heaven on earth. Renouncement of our fleshy and earthly desires, renouncing the selfishness first that is permitted to reside in our own homes, is the way in which we most directly beckon "Thy kingdom *come*," ushering in and preparing the way for the King of kings (Daniel 2:37; Revelation 17:14).

Unable to discern the difference between "thy" and "my," my then two-year-old daughter would frequently pray "my will be done." How wise she really was regarding human nature. Indeed, wisdom pours forth out of the mouths of babes (Psalm

**The Living Word often uttered words that cut deeply.**

8:2-3). Sadly, though, many of us never grow out of this childish approach to God's created world. The Lord's Prayer challenges us to ask tough questions en route to a greater love for God, namely, "Do you live each day in an effort to build God's kingdom or your own?" It's easier to carry on with our selfishness when we think we're pulling the wool over the Shepherd's eyes. Scripture reminds us that he sees everything we do (Job 34:21; Psalm 33:13), a truth that should cut us more deeply than any sword (Hebrews 4:12). The Living Word often uttered words that cut deeply. Always steeped in love, Christ's words were an invitation to **renounce** the finite kingdom in favor of his infinite one.

## *The poorest rich man on the planet*

How dejected the young man must have felt as he walked away. Wealthy, confident, and well-bred, he thought he had the world on a string when he rose to ask the wise carpenter a question. He knew the commandments well. His question and response revealed that he knew the letter of the law but not the Author of it. The kingdom he was expecting to come with the Messiah was crumbling around him, as Christ offered him an invitation to die to all he held dear. St. Mark gives us the story of this rich young man in chapter ten:

> And as he was setting out on his journey, a man ran up and knelt before him, and asked him, "Good Teacher, what must I do to inherit eternal life?" And Jesus said to him, "Why do you call me good? No one is good but God alone. You know the commandments: 'Do not kill, Do not commit adultery, Do not steal, Do not bear false witness, Do not defraud, Honor your father and mother.'" And he said to him, "Teacher, all these I have observed from my youth." And Jesus looking upon him loved him, and said to him, "You lack one thing; go, sell what you have, and give to the poor, and you will have treasure in heaven; and come, follow me." At that saying his countenance fell, and he went away sorrowful; for he had great possessions. (Mark 10:17-22)

Now, to be clear, this question he poses to Jesus, "What must I do to inherit eternal life?" is not the same as the question we ask, "Lord, what must I do to go to heaven?" The young man was asking a Jewish question to a Jewish teacher. He was under the obligation of the Torah, which Jesus quoted to him. His question wasn't about heavenly treasures as much as it was about "his share" of the kingdom. He believed that the kingdom would come when God sent the Messiah and destroyed the other kingdoms of the world. He was envisioning a new earthly kingdom coming in majesty, and this young go-getter wanted in. Christ's response is one of "good news/bad news." The good news is that the young man could taste the heavenly kingdom; the bad news is that it was going to cost him his earthly kingdom. Jesus' response to him is the same as his invitation to us: **renounce**.

Jesus discussed the need to leave behind riches with other people too, but not as emphatically as he seemed to with this specific young man. Telling him to sell all of his earthly possessions (**renouncement**) is equivalent to challenging the young man to forsake all of his false gods, his earthly idols of material pleasure or cultural esteem. Christ was trying to free him from the ties that bind, from a love of possessions or money that is "the root of all evils" (1 Timothy 6:10). As Robert Browning said, "Ah, but one's reach should exceed one's grasp or what's heaven for?"

Like the rich young man, we live in a culture of immediate gratification and material desire. We like our stuff. We get attached to our stuff. Jesus knew something we too quickly forget, namely, that our earthly possessions get in the way of our ultimate goal. Possessions weren't keeping this young man from God; the love that he had for possessions *before God* was keeping him out. That was the sin.

Christianity teaches us total surrender. It invites us to abandon everything of this world in favor of the next. Now, this is not to say that we are all called into monastic life—God's desire is not for each of us to live like ascetics. This is to say that we must strive to be freed from the slavery that often accompanies material things. As St. John reminds us, we must be in the world but not "of the world" (John 15:19). We must be willing to surrender our own plans and control—even over our finances—and allow God to be at the center of our lives. In putting our money where

## "In God we trust" should be our motto, not our money's.

our mouth is, tithing is no longer "optional." "In God we trust" should be our motto, not our money's. It doesn't mean we cannot have or delight in nice things, only that we can never allow them to become gods—to allow our "kingdoms" to become primary rather than God's kingdom. This type of **renouncement** is not easy and cannot be partial.

The rich young man was invited not only to sell his possessions but, more important, to abandon his *previous understanding* of the kingdom of God. He was being invited to be part of a New Israel, where Jesus, not the Torah, was the center of teaching and life. His goal wasn't God's goal, and God offered him clarity. In order to embrace this radical **renouncement** of what he held dear, he needed to remember one thing: that "God made us for himself; he made us for heaven."[9] God offers us the same reminder, invitation, and challenge he offered the young man, each and every time we pray "Thy kingdom come."

Many of the great saints started out quite rich, including St. Augustine, St. Clare, and St. Patrick, to name a few. Bearing that in mind, how many died rich? How many rich saints can you name? Again, this is not to say that people with money will not taste heaven, only that to whom more is given, more is expected (Luke 12:48). If our love for money outweighs our love for the kingdom, we're working for the wrong master. If I am not willing to **renounce** all that I have, the kingdom I seek is mine, not thine.

## Responding to This Petition

### *How does his kingdom become my kingdom?*

Take the time to reflect on the issues below. They will help you discover when you are living for God's kingdom or when you are living for your own.

- What role does the Lord play in your finances? Do you tithe when both the economy is strong *and* when your personal finances are struggling? It's less about the gross amount than it is about the sacrifice, as evidenced in stories like the widow's mite (Luke 21:1-4). Have you renounced the need to store up too much wealth for "comfort" or security while others go without? What can you do to insure that the Lord is the Lord of your finances?

- What role does the Lord play in your dating relationships and/or marriage? What steps do you take to insure that a spouse (or prospective spouse) is also seeking God's kingdom over his/her own? Does your marriage or dating relationship revolve around what you get from it or what you give to it?

- What role does the Lord play in your sexuality? Do you live chastely, regardless of your state? (To be sure, chastity is a virtue for all, married and unmarried alike.) If you are married, have you renounced artificial means of preventing conception and allowed the Lord to be the Lord of your bedroom as well?

- What role does the Lord play in your familial relationships? How is an attitude of service, like that to which the Lord calls us (Matthew 23:11; John 13:5), displayed in your home? How is the Lord's kingdom made manifest in your family room, kitchen, and living room? How does your child rearing reflect the Lord's kingdom over your own? Do you seek to control your children or raise them as God's children? In what ways does your home reflect a home of loving purpose and divine service (Joshua 24:15)?

- What role does the Lord play in your professional occupation? Each of your talents and skills comes from him. Have you used these talents and skills for his glory or for your own? Even if you pulled yourself up from your own bootstraps, your work ethic and perseverance are gifts from the Father. Have you been a good steward of these gifts (1 Peter

4:10), using them for God's glory or for your own prestige, advancement, popularity, or positioning?

- What role does the Lord play in your future? Do you open yourself up, daily, in prayer, inviting the Lord into your best laid plans for the next five to fifty years? How have you let God into *your planning* for the future, be it education, occupation, vocation, or retirement?

- How do you invite the Lord into your personal fears and insecurities? What active steps do you take to face fears, admit struggles, and reach out to God, beckoning *his kingdom* to come crashing into your own world each day?

- In short, ask yourself the following question each morning when you wake up and each night when you retire: Did my day today reflect what is most important in God's eyes or the world's? The answer to that question goes a long way in determining whose kingdom is being announced and whose was being renounced.

The kingdom of God is at hand. Some are working for it; others are working for their own kingdom. Only you and God know which one you're building every day, and only you and God will account for it on your final day. **Renouncement** is difficult but worth more than any wealth we can amass on earth.

Now, if we're going to move on in this prayer, we must come to grips with this reality: that as we let go of our own kingdoms, we must be ready to embrace God's kingdom as he wills it.

## Questions for Reflection and Discussion

1. What are some of the ways or people by which God has invited you to rethink your life and renounce your own "kingdoms"?

2. In order for God's kingdom to come into our daily lives, our miniature kingdoms must go. Does this concept leave you fearful or free? Do you truly desire God's kingdom—and all that comes with it—to come?

3. Going back to the question posed midchapter: Do you live each day in an effort to build God's kingdom or your own? Explain, using concrete examples.

4. What is the most difficult worldly thing for you to renounce? Is it financial security, clothes, gadgets, or something else? If your loved ones were safe, what's the first thing you'd try to "save" in a fire? Is it difficult to let that thing go? Explain.

# CHAPTER SEVEN

# "Thy Will Be Done"

## REAFFIRMING Whose Will We Seek

Taken, blessed, broken, and shared. It was a formula the disciples had seen before, when Jesus fed the multitudes. It was the formula again during the Passover meal that Thursday night, but its effects would prove eternal. The cup was put down and the sandals retied. Scripture tells us the meal ended with a hymn of praise. Shortly following, Christ and the remaining eleven made their way from the upper room to the Garden of Gethsemane, nestled on the Mount of Olives.

Just as our relationship with God had begun in a garden, our relationship with God would now be set straight in a garden. Gethsemane was the location of the olive press on Mount Olivet, where purveyors would extract the precious oil from often precocious fruit; Gethsemane literally means "the place of crushing," an appropriate name for the events that would soon transpire there.

God had walked with Adam in a garden. God and man had another rendezvous in the late night hours on Holy Thursday. Although flanked by soldiers and the betrayer Judas, Christ left the garden alone, without those who had promised to remain with him, even to die with him (Matthew 26:35). That walk to the house of Caiaphas was a solo walk, as was the walk that would later culminate in a cross, a hill of skulls, and the ultimate sacrifice on the afternoon of Good Friday. Following God's will is often filled with loneliness, abandonment, suffering, and betrayal. Sadly, it's no walk in a garden.

Christ's prayer reminds us that love is far more than a feeling; love is a decision. If true love were only about feelings, Jesus would have been hugged to death for our redemption. Suffering is part of love. The word "passion" comes from the Latin *pati,* which means "to suffer." Pope Benedict XVI has reminded us that "when we come to consider Jesus' passion, we will need to focus explicitly on this prayer, in which Jesus gives us a glimpse into his human soul and its 'becoming-one' with the will of God."[10]

It was against this backdrop of a garden, a location where (through his pride) man had chosen himself over God, that the God-man would choose to be selfless for all mankind. It was at this time that Christ chose to drink from a far different cup:

> And going a little farther he fell on his face and prayed, "My Father, if it be possible, let this chalice pass from me; nevertheless, not as I will, but as thou will." (Matthew 26:39)

We know those words. We proclaim them every time we pray the Lord's Prayer. We ponder the scene every Lent. If we listen closely enough, we can even hear the words as a resounding echo of the words from our Lord's mother at the annunciation: "Be it done to me *according to thy will*" (see Luke 1:38). If we wish to comprehend Jesus' words, we must first comprehend his mother's, which Mary not only said but lived. Mary's perfect faithfulness paved the way for God to accomplish his will through her. Jesus' life and his prayer become one ongoing sacrifice, echoing the prayer and sacrifice of the Blessed Mother, who **reaffirmed** to him, her community, and all of humanity God's supremacy and lordship in her own life.

> **Mary's perfect faithfulness paved the way for God to accomplish his will through her.**

Do these words change your life? They changed Jesus' life. They certainly changed Mary's life. They have changed the lives of countless martyrs and believers since our heavenly Mother and Savior first uttered them. But do they change *your* life? Are these the words you pray? Is this the battle cry of surrender that begins and ends your day? Too often, for me, the answer is no.

### The (Last) Will and (New) Testament

The Garden of Gethsemane might seem thousands of miles away, but it's not. We all have our own Gethsemanes, our own places of crushing, where we have the choice of our will over the Father's. For some reading this, your home is a minor Gethsemane, where you are given the opportunity for total selflessness daily. For others, your Gethsemane has a water cooler, copier, and cubicle walls. Offices are often places of crushing where we discern how much we are willing to undergo to "pay the price" of mortgages, debt, college tuition, and life. For some souls thumbing through these pages, your relationships are Gethsemanes, places of fear or loneliness, where you feel like others you depend on have fallen asleep or are with you physically but not emotionally (Matthew 26:40, 43).

While everyone's story is different, the collective struggle is the same—namely, "Do I really trust God enough to put my wants, comforts, goals, desires, and plans aside in favor of his plan *for me*? Am I not only able but *willing* to drink from his cup?"

### Reaffirmation—checking the GPS

I was in my car facing a brick wall. The GPS said to drive forward. Doing so would have resulted in both a cracked radiator and skull. I sat indignant behind the wheel. I'd spent *that much* on a GPS that told me to drive into a wall? I was so annoyed, and on top of that, I was lost.

The GPS is programmed to get us to our destination. Mine failed. God's doesn't. God's GPS is hardwired into our con-

> **God's GPS is the Holy Spirit. If we heeded the directions offered through him, we'd get to heaven.**

science. God's GPS is the Holy Spirit. If we heeded the directions offered through him, we'd get to heaven. The only problem is that the route the Holy Spirit gives us is often not the route we'd select for ourselves. We prefer a route that is shorter, faster, and smoother. We attempt to program our route through life without any thought to growth, suffering, or virtue. In short, we choose the path of least resistance and call it a day. Few if any of us would route our life through Gethsemane.

This prayer, however, "Thy will be done," **reaffirms** that the quickest and easiest path is often not the one that leads to our desired destination. No, the easy path is often a detour from grace to sin. God's path is not the easy path. Although his yoke is easy and his burden light (Matthew 11:30), the path of righteousness is beset on all sides by difficulty and temptation. When Christ gave us the beatitudes (Matthew 5:1-9), he **reaffirmed** to us that God's path is not what the GPS will come up with; God's life is not a life most seek to live out. His teaching **reaffirms** that oftentimes his will is sadly not our will.

Daily the Christian walk invites us to reexamine our goals, vows, priorities, and lifestyle. God invites us to new levels of sacrifice with the purpose of affirming and (for us) **reaffirming** his lordship over all creation. God's desire is not that we devalue ourselves. God's desire is that we view our worth through the lens of his love. We are only breathing because of him. We do not sustain our existence on our own. If God stopped thinking about us for a nanosecond, we would cease to exist. He is sustaining our lives—your life—at this very moment. Our adherence to his will and genuine joy in seeking it are a **reaffirmation** to him that we not only acknowledge his supremacy but relish it.

### The cost of sainthood

A saint gives God permission to remove anything and anyone from his life that keeps him from sainthood.

That sentence cost nothing to write. It is eighteen words, several dozen characters—it's a line or so of ink in a mass-produced book. Those eighteen words are shared freely; they cost me nothing to say but they cost everything to live. They **reaffirm** "Thy will be done" in a bold and practical way. If you pray this prayer every day with sincerity, your life will change. Praying just this prayer every day is worth the cost of this book. Living that prayer daily is the toughest challenge any of us could ever face.

This is the life that Christ led. This is the prayer of Mary's heart. This is what it means to be a true disciple. This is what it means to follow God with your whole life: that every decision be made according to God's will for you, not according to your level of comfort, the path of least resistance, popular opinion, or political correctness. Sainthood means that his will becomes the motivating factor for all your decisions. God's will becomes the breath you breathe, the mind-set you adopt, the plan you employ, and the blueprint you follow. This is the saints' playbook for eternal life (Matthew 7:21). The more you live it and pray it, the more you **reaffirm** it, both to yourself, to your God, and to the world. The world needs this humble boldness from its Christians. Our love must "invert" the world more than subvert it (Acts 17:6).

God's will is not something you take off the shelf on Sundays or the lens you look through when tough moral decisions demand a verdict. No, God's will is like an eye transplant that allows you, possibly for the first time ever, to actually see 20/20. God's will must be our solitary goal, irrevocably intertwined with our very essence. When we live to do God's will, as the saints do, we submit to the reality of Christ who looked upon "the unity of his will with the Father's will (as) the core of his very being."[11]

This unity of wills is a portrait of sanctity, the perfection of charity by which we synchronize our hearts to his Sacred Heart. It's this faithfulness in serving the Master, *by fulfilling his will over our own*, that he rewards, not with "more work," but with more of his trust (Matthew 25:23). Our yes to God is a **reaffirmation** of Christ's yes and of his mother's *fiat*.


## Responding to This Petition

### *Sainthood in the suburbs*

A great way to "practice" putting our will and our own desires aside is to change our perspective and our disciplines for a few weeks. Create a list of all the everyday or monthly "things" you dislike doing. It can be long or short, detailed or broadstroked, as long as you put pen to paper and write it out. Seeing it in your own handwriting is important because it's from this list that you are going to begin your journey toward true holiness. Something as seemingly inane as making your bed each day (if that's what you loathe most) can help you achieve sainthood through discipline and sacrifice.

Speaking for myself, there were several activities when I was growing up that I disliked intensely: reading books, doing homework, washing the dishes, mowing the lawn, going to church. They were just a few of the things I dreaded most on the average day or week. God has a funny way of using time, however, to change our perspective on things.

Now I'm older and (hopefully) wiser. And now that I'm a husband and father, I barely have time to tie my shoes or read the paper. Life is no longer about what I "want" to do with my free time but what I "need" to do with it. Now I get excited to read—much less finish—a book. Now I actually look forward to elementary-school homework, because it is more time I get to spend with my daughter. Now I don't mind washing the dishes, because it means I don't have to change the dirty diapers that come right after dinner. It also reminds me of how fortunate we are to have food to eat each day. I still hate mowing the lawn, so we moved to the desert. Now, not only do I look forward to Mass, but I yearn for that intimate time with our Lord each day at Mass. Some would say that the tasks have changed with parenthood. Some would say that my perspective has changed. Both are correct, but there is a deeper reality going on within me. *God is changing me* through his grace. He's changing you too.

Every time that we do something we don't particularly "want" to do, out of our love for God or out of obedience, there is grace.

> **God is changing me through his grace. He's changing you too.**

Every time we put others' needs before our own in humble acts of service, there is grace. Every time we endure hardship for the sake of our vocation, the gospel, or the Church, there is grace. Truly embracing your vocation means embracing what God wants you to do each day, not what you "feel like" doing. It means putting God, not you, first. Living this lifestyle reaffirms who you are by **reaffirming** *whose* you are. There is no small sacrifice, no meaningless mortification, in the eyes of God.

As for that list of things you don't like to do? Read it again. Identify those things, acknowledge them, and then do them anyway. There is grace in doing the things you don't want to do. God is so generous that he even pours out additional graces when you offer up those tasks on behalf of other people's welfare and sanctification. In the character and the humility you derive from such tasks, the Lord refines you and prepares you in time for even greater tasks (Matthew 25:21). Scripture affirms that God's grace is enough; it is sufficient (2 Corinthians 12:9) and free (Romans 5:17). Your actions will **reaffirm** your beliefs while **reaffirming** whose will it is that you truly seek.

### More listening than talking

On a practical level, how do we know if we are *really seeking* God's will and not our own? It takes discernment, and discernment takes prayer. If you never pray, true discernment of his will for your life probably won't come from one ten-minute "rap session" with God. No, for most of us, authentically discerning God's will takes more listening than talking. We seek answers from God but are seldom silent enough to hear anything. God gave you two ears and one mouth; use them proportionally. This constant communication is what St. Paul calls prayer (1 Thessalonians 5:17), and it's the secret to a peaceful life.

Prayer is more than an inner monologue. Prayer is a dialogue in which you learn about love. Prayer isn't about changing other people; prayer is about changing your own heart. The more we pray, the better we can know and discern "thy will," the will of God. Our lives are supposed to **reaffirm** God's plan for us, not our own.

When you're sitting in your Garden of Gethsemane, whose cup are you drinking from? Are you drinking from your own cup or the Lord's cup? Some days his cup is filled with joyful abundance and other days with suffering and hardship. Are you willing to take the bad with the good, or are you looking to avoid suffering at all costs? Are you missing out on the cup of peace and life for fear that it will become a cup of loneliness and betrayal? Are you drinking from the cup of surrender and humility, **reaffirming**

> **Never miss an opportunity to reaffirm, in big and small ways, who God is.**

that God's will is more important than your own? Never miss an opportunity to **reaffirm**, in big and small ways, who God is.

How do we learn to discern, follow, teach, and seek God's will in all situations? Jesus cared enough about us to give us the answer before he left the earth.

## Questions for Reflection and Discussion

1. When has following God's will (over the world's way) caused you suffering? Try to name a specific instance. How did this affect your relationship with God?

2. As was stated in this chapter, answer the following question: Do I really trust God enough to put my wants, comforts, goals, desires, and plans aside in favor of his plan *for me*? Am I not only able but *willing* to drink from his cup? Why or why not?

3. Name a time that your desire for the "quick and easy" path led to greater frustration, suffering, or an unwanted end. How could you avoid such an outcome in the future?

4. What role does prayer play in your important decisions? What role does prayer play in the smaller, daily, seemingly "insignificant" decisions? Is there a difference? Discuss.

5. How is God changing you through his grace? Give some examples.

# CHAPTER EIGHT

# "On Earth as It Is in Heaven"

# The Opportunity for

# REMEMBRANCE

We've already discussed heaven and how it needs to be our goal. So, you might be asking, what more need be said about this topic of heaven? In this line of the Lord's Prayer, we're just praying that God's will be done *more perfectly* on earth, right? Isn't that the basic gist of it? But how can we do his will on earth the way it's done in heaven if we don't *first* head to heaven for a new perspective on earth? And how does a Catholic see heaven?

### *Massive boredom*

The midweek teen Bible study was being held in the parish youth room. Fluorescent lights buzzed overhead, and the smell of burnt popcorn filled the air. A handful of teens sat attentively on gaudy, heavily worn couches donated by parishioners. Other teens, less than enthused by the subject matter, were falling asleep. Oblivious to how I had lost their attention, I nervously followed my notes and continued. I was the new youth minister, and not a very good one.

"So, as you can clearly see in the Book of Revelation, the Catholic Mass is a foretaste of heaven. When we go to Mass, it's like we're getting a glimpse of heaven. That's what heaven is like—it's like when we worship God at Mass," I said proudly.

There was a stunned silence in the room (I presumed because of the brilliance of my assertions and the clarity with which I had articulated the incommunicable glory of heaven). The silence filled my soul with a bit of vainglory. I had finally done it—I had left the teens speechless through my catechesis. It was at that moment that the silence was shattered with brutal honesty.

A teen named Danny looked me straight in the eye and with a disheartened tone said, "If heaven is like Mass, I'd rather go to hell." The mood in the room suddenly shifted, and the teens laughed nervously, some nodding in agreement. He had struck a nerve, and his response was honest. I've always appreciated the authenticity of teenagers, especially regarding matters of faith. They're willing to say things that some adults are only courageous enough to think.

My failure as a Bible-study leader and youth minister was not because I was boring or because I couldn't get the teens enthused about the Mass, although, to be quite honest, both were true. I was failing because *I* was not enthused. The problem wasn't with the body but with the head (John 10:12), the shepherd, not the flock.

I dutifully attended Mass, most of the time out of obligation rather than desire. The liturgy was often painful—bad music, irrelevant homilies, and a congregation that seemed barely alive. I began a Bible study knowing little to nothing about Scripture. I did it because I thought it was what I was supposed to do. I was working about one week ahead of the teens. Looking back, I was leading them to confusion, not to Christ.

Things changed the day that Danny spoke up. I finished the study that night, drove home, and was humbled to the point of tears. Where had I gone wrong? I knew the history of the Mass. I knew the prayers, the petitions, and the purpose of it. That night it hit me: I didn't desire that reunion with my Father in heaven because I had yet to really comprehend my union, and my communion, with him on earth. Every single Mass, he was offering to become one with me—to "re-member" me—as I received the Eucharist, to become one member, again and again, with him.

### Prayers equals purpose

The Mass is not intended to entertain us but to enrapture us. Mass is a full contact sport, not a spectator sport, but most of the time, we just don't understand the action transpiring before our eyes. I hear a lot of Catholics grumble about their experience at Mass. Some complain about the music but most complain about the preaching. They base their entire experience of the Mass on the homily. If the homily is uninspiring, they leave uninspired. Ironically, that's one of the reasons I adore the Catholic faith.

Our experience of God on Sunday isn't dependent but transcendent. If the preaching stinks or the music ministry is so bad that the neighborhood cats flee in fear, it matters little in the grand

> **Our experience of God on Sunday isn't dependent but transcendent.**

scheme of things. I still receive Jesus Christ in the Eucharist, the word, the priesthood, and the assembly of believers. Sure, I'd love a great homily and music that would make the angelic host stand

and take notice, but more important than those things—which we ought always to strive for, since God deserves our best—is the fact that the God of heaven and earth is reaching down and lifting us up into his throne room for an hour, giving us a glimpse and a foretaste of heaven. As Catholics in the mystical body of Christ, we are privileged to enjoy an intimate encounter with the eternal presence of Jesus Christ—body, blood, soul, and divinity— upon the altar as our focal point.

The Mass, first and foremost, is a sacrifice. For this reason, it's no wonder that many don't fully comprehend or appreciate the beautiful reality of what is transpiring in the sanctuary. Sacrifice is a foreign and at times almost dirty word in the culture of "I," but "sacrifice is part of what it means to be truly human."[12]

### Remember the sacrifice

When we speak of "sacrifice" in our modern, technologically savvy culture, it has a distinctly different meaning than it did for most generations past. For us, sacrifice entails working a second job, going without that new gadget or pedicure until the next paycheck, buying the generic brand, or giving up the remote control. When we talk about what we sacrifice in America, it's normally in this more metaphorical sense. Few of us have ever witnessed the sacrifice of an animal, for instance, and if we did, at some point during the bloodletting and disemboweling, we would agree that, as twenty-first century Christians in first-world countries, we play fast and loose with the word.

The Scripture scholar and Anglican bishop N. T. Wright summed up sacrifice beautifully in his book *Following Jesus*, saying:

The temptation we humans face, which Jesus faced in the wilderness, is to snatch at the world to use it for our own pleasure or glory. But when we bring a symbol of the created world before the creator God in gratitude and offering, we are symbolically saying that he is the creator, and that we have no rights over creation independently of him. To that extent, sacrifice is the natural and appropriate human activity.[13]

Sacrifice publicly demonstrates not only our need for God but our acknowledgment of who God is and who we are not. Sacrifice is difficult for a culture of self-sufficient self-starters; it requires

> **Sacrifice helps us put and keep God in the center of our lives.**

humility to acknowledge God's primacy and our need for him. Sacrifice helps us put and keep God in the center of our lives. This is one of the reasons that the Catholic Church doesn't just have us gather to sing or tell stories on Sunday but that she bids us to come together for worship and *remembrance* of the sacrifice of Christ.

Jesus' command was "Do this in remembrance of me" (Luke 22:19). The word "remembrance" means more than to "recollect." Jesus wasn't saying, "Hey, guys, after I'm gone, why don't you all get together and reminisce. Tell some funny stories, sing some songs, check in with one another because accountability is important, and then, you know, 'remember' me. Just think about all the good times we had." No, this new covenant would fulfill what the prophet Jeremiah had foretold seven hundred years prior (Jeremiah 31:31-34). In this new and everlasting covenant, we would **"re-member"** Christ—become one member with him, again—through the living bread of his living body (John 6:35, 48, 51, 53-56). This was no misunderstanding, for even St. Paul, not present in the upper room that night, confessed twenty years later that the tradition was handed on to him orally (1 Corinthians 11:23-26).

Through the Eucharist, Christ **remembers** us as he promised (Matthew 28:20), and in doing so renews our relationship with the Father, again and again. It's in this moment after receiving the God of the universe in his most Blessed Sacrament, more than at any other time in the course of our week, that things are finally *on earth as they are in heaven.* It's for this reason, as well, that St. Paul warns us against receiving Christ's body and blood if we are not in a state of grace (1 Corinthians 11:27-29); our souls ought to be properly disposed and prepared to become walking tabernacles if we walk forward to receive him. Christ sacrificed for us. It is the understatement of a lifetime to say that the least we can do is reconcile any serious sin before he humbles himself to **re-member** us and consume us with his love, as we **re-member** and consume him.

We should all desire to see and hear the Mass, not from an earthly perspective, but from a heavenly one. The Mass is the re-presentation of Christ's timeless, once-and-for-all sacrifice (see *Catechism of the Catholic Church*, 1366), meaning that at every single Mass, we are present in the upper room with Christ (in the person of the priest), at the table for the Last Supper. At every single Mass, we are present at Calvary, to witness the greatest

display of perfect love the world has ever seen, for the cross "is
love in its most radical form."[14]

Sometimes to get a better view of what's happening on earth,
we need to view earth from heaven. That's the vision God gave to
St. John in the Book of Revelation. God lifted him up to heaven
so that he might see things from a broader, more divine perspective. When we read Revelation, then, we are getting a "God's-eye"
view of ourselves, of our worship, and of our ultimate end.

### Beginning with the end in mind

The Book of Revelation is one of the most talked about books
in the entire Bible. For centuries scholars have debated it, extract-
ing from its pages every conceivable meaning from every symbol,
number, allegory, and phrase. Entire belief systems have been
based on just a few words, taken out of context here or there.

Revelation describes a series of visions that St. John experienced, which pointed to the *parousia,* the second coming of
Christ. Many over the past two thousand years have interpreted
Revelation solely through a "futurist" perspective—one that
believes John's visions were solely about the final judgment that
has yet to occur. Others have seen Revelation as a dramatization
of the spiritual life or believe that it represents successive stages
of Church history through time. Still others have viewed it solely
through a "preterist" perspective that believes most, if not all, of
the events described in Revelation happened within the lives of
the original readers of the book. Each view has its advantages,
and the whole truth probably contains aspects of each.[15]

A closer examination of the word "parousia," however, reveals
something interesting in that the word doesn't just mean "second

coming" but more literally, "presence." While most of the prophecies in Revelation have been fulfilled through Jesus Christ (and in the ongoing expansion of his kingdom), the early Church fathers also believed Revelation to be about the eternal presence of Christ, the way in which Jesus Christ "comes" into our midst regularly, most specifically through the Catholic Mass.

The ancient title for the Book of Revelation is *Apokalypsis*, which literally means "pull back the veil." This is wedding imagery. Just as marriage is used as a symbolic element throughout Scripture, the final chapters of Revelation actually depict a wedding liturgy. Rather than being a book to fear, Revelation is a book filled with hope. St. Augustine said we could understand the words "Thy will be done on earth as it is in heaven" to mean: "in the Church as in our Lord Jesus Christ himself"; or "in the Bride [the Church] who has been betrothed, just as in the Bridegroom [Christ] who has accomplished the will of the Father" (*Catechism of the Catholic Church*, 2827).

### Crashing the heavenly wedding

The truth is that God himself is the author of marriage (see *Catechism of the Catholic Church*, 1603). It was not a government or court that gave us marriage; it was our Creator. At the very beginning, we see the foundation of the sacrament (Genesis 2:18). Notice that I didn't say "contract," because marriage is more than a contract; marriage is a covenant. A covenant is more than a legal formality or an exchange of goods and services. It involves total surrender and total self-gift, a relationship entered into with God.

Christ, the groom, has proposed to the Church, his bride. The ring, the promise of his eternal and undying love, is the new covenant. Through the sacraments, we (the Church) achieve the greatest possible physical intimacy with Christ. Why all this imagery of marriage? Why the analogy of the bride and groom? Why is this the example through which God wants to teach us about our relationship to him?

He who does not love does not know God; for God is love. (1 John 4:8)

It's that simple: God is love. As perfect love, God desires to share that perfect love. Thanks to the cross and through baptism, we are invited into that love in an intimate way. We are not

> **As perfect love, God desires to share that perfect love.**

just clay in the hands of a potter. We are not just animals with an owner. We are not, even, just slaves with a master. We are called into an intimate relationship, that of a pure lover, in which we can become one with God and bear fruit in his name. Consider this line from the closing chapters of Revelation:

"Let us rejoice and exult and give him the glory, / for the marriage of the Lamb has come, / and his Bride has made herself ready; / it was granted her to be clothed with fine linen, bright and pure. . . . / *Blessed are those who are invited to the marriage supper of the Lamb.*" (Revelation 19:7-9; emphasis added)

As has already been stated, Scripture uses wedding imagery early and often, as an allegory to teach us about God's love for us. Christ is the bridegroom (Revelation 19:6-13; John 3:29; Ephesians 5:23). The Church—you and I and everyone who is baptized—is his bride. Now I realize that this may be an extremely uncomfortable concept for the male reader, but stay with me, because the metaphor of the Church as the bride and Christ as the bridegroom is foundational to our understanding of Christ's intimate and eternal presence with us. If it reflects the reality, as Scripture affirms in passages like the one above and in many others (Ephesians 5:21-33; Matthew 22:1-14), then our entire understanding of the Mass needs to be transformed into one of a wedding liturgy.

## Responding to This Petition

### *Before you say "I do"*

As we are reminded, before we receive the Eucharist, the state of our souls ought be "white as snow" (Isaiah 1:18). God gives us a true gift, allowing our mortal sins to be forgiven and allowing us to be transformed by his grace in the Sacrament of Reconciliation—this is how we are adorned in the "fine linen, bright and pure" referred to in Revelation 19:8. As we, the faithful bride, walk down the aisle to meet our groom, clothed in a tuxedo that looks and tastes like bread, we hear the words "The body of Christ." That proclamation deserves *and demands* a response. In this moment, Christ and his bride personify **remembrance,** becoming one once again.

On my wedding day, I stood before my bride and offered her not only my body but my being. I was not offering her a house in the suburbs, a joint checking account, a shared philosophy on raising children, and cute Christmas card pictures for life. I was offering her my very life. In the exchange of vows, before an altar of God and a priest of God in the house of God, I was offering her all of myself. Her response to my proposal for the two of us to become one was "I do." That night after the wedding, I offered my bride my body and she offered me hers, as we consummated our new covenant through a total self-gift on both of our parts.

The beautiful intimacy shared by a man and woman in the Sacrament of Matrimony and in the marital act is outshone only by the intimacy offered to every Catholic (in a state of grace) when they come forward to receive Christ's body and blood in the Eucharist. "The word 'intimacy' comes from *intus*, which means 'within.' God is intimate with us . . . [as] he promised to dwell within us (John 14:17)."[16]

## The veil is being lifted during Communion. The bride and groom are becoming one.

As we, the bride, approach Christ, the groom, we respond to his invitation for the two to become one with our "I do," a simple "Amen," meaning "Yes, I believe." Our acknowledgment and proclamation signify humble acceptance, with a vow attached. It's in the moment that we consume the host that we'd be wise to **remember** what is happening; the words "consume" and "consummate" share the same root word in Latin. The veil is being lifted during Communion. The bride and groom are becoming one. Each time my wife and I come together in the marital act, we renew our marital vows. Each time you receive the Eucharist, you are renewing your baptismal vows to God, pledging to forsake all other "lovers" and lusts of this world in favor of him and his undying love.

When we receive Christ's flesh in the Eucharist, we are finally fulfilling his directive to "do this in **remembrance**" (Luke 22:19). We are no longer members of the body of Christ, figuratively or symbolically, but physically and ethereally. *This* is how "heaven and earth are filled with his glory," as we proclaim with joy at every liturgy. *This* is how we worship God *on earth as it is in heaven*, by being in communion with him. It's at *this moment*, empowered by his grace, that we are sent forth (Mass comes from the word *missio,* meaning "to be sent forth") to go out into a world plagued with sin and to love it back into the Father's arms. The two have become one, just as Jesus foretold (Matthew 19:6). After consummating our relationship in perfect **remembrance**, the holy couple now go forth to bear fruit, to bring life to a culture of death and proclaim hope to a world tainted with sickness, depression, and death.

Of course, that's the view from heaven, but we still have needs on earth. We still have physical bodies with physical appetites. We are hungry and thirsty . . . but for what?

Worship reveals the dehydration of our souls. It seeks the "living water" (John 7:38)

## Questions for Reflection and Discussion

1. Consider what three adjectives you would use to describe your normal experience of the Mass. Share them aloud.

2. Is the imagery of the Mass as a wedding liturgy a new concept for you? If so, what thoughts and feelings does it evoke within you? If not, how does this reality translate to your Mass-going experience each day or week? Explain.

3. On a scale of one to ten, rate the intimacy of your relationship to Christ. Explain why you chose that number and how that intimacy could possibly grow.

4. How does the bride—the Church—"bear fruit" for the world after consummating her relationship with Christ (the bridegroom) at every Mass?

5. What are two tangible things that you can do this week to be more present to the Lord during Mass?

# CHAPTER NINE

# "Give Us This Day Our Daily Bread"
## The Necessity of **RELIANCE**

I t's at this moment within the Lord's Prayer that our desire and tone change. By change, I don't mean to suggest that we are in any way losing our focus on God the Father, but instead we are switching gears within the petitions.

Thus far, we have concentrated on worshipping and adoring God for who he is—our Father, wholly present and holy. We have praised his holy name and beseeched that his kingdom and his will be done perfectly, throughout all of creation. It's at this point that we direct the desires of our hearts to God. We bless him by stating, publicly, our needs and our **reliance** on him. By doing so, we grow deeper into his image, pursuing the "crown of righteousness" that St. Paul talked about (2 Timothy 4:8).

When most Catholics hear "daily bread," they automatically think of the Eucharist, and rightly so. The Eucharist is the source and summit of our faith (see *Catechism of the Catholic Church*, 1328–34). In other words, our entire faith not only flows from the Eucharist (the source) but also flows toward it (the summit). This is one of the greatest of mysteries—not a mystery to solve but a mystery to behold. Faith does not contradict reason; it exceeds it. And while we can never do justice to the depth, breadth, truth, or importance of the holy Eucharist in just a few pages, it is vital to note that when we pray "Give us this day our daily bread," we are praying for far more than God's Eucharistic presence. Daily bread speaks to our needs, our hunger, and ultimately our **reliance** on God, physically and spiritually, every moment of the day.

### The family dinner table

The dinner table in our home is what I like to call "a display of unholy holiness." Interruptions are commonplace. Bathroom breaks seem almost inevitable. Voice volume increases steadily, not because of anger, but out of a sheer desire to be heard. Sitting there, surrounded by my wife and three young daughters, I am filled with stress (many nights) and joy (all nights). I am truly blessed to be the father of this beautiful family and to be called to provide for their needs.

And what are their needs? They need a home. They need food. They need clothes. My daughters even need a repairman for their Barbie playhouse. Even more important than all of these needs, however, is the need my family has for a holy father, one who doesn't just care *for them*, but one who cares *about them*. A house is where earthly stuff is stored. A home is where heavenly stuff is taught, lived, and learned. The hunger my girls experience goes far beyond the cries of their stomachs; it's a hunger that comes from their souls. Children are created with a natural **reliance** on their parents. When we do not establish the proper parent-child relationship at an early age, or if we rush them to self-reliance too soon, we inhibit their spiritual maturity down the road. While the world expects us to become increasingly self-reliant and responsible, heaven desires that we become increasingly dependent and childlike the older we get (Mark 10:13-16).

As we've already spoken about, earthly fathers are supposed to be mirrors of the heavenly Father's love. If more husbands and fathers would put as much energy into their marriages and families as they do their jobs, the world would change. The sooner my children believe that their earthly father wants good things for them—that I care *about them* and not just *for them*—the easier the ultimate transition will be for my kids to trust that their heavenly Father also wants good things for them (Matthew 7:7-11). God's desire is that we go to him for everything, and then trust that he will fulfill our needs in accordance with *his will* (as discussed in chapter seven). Part of trusting that God will not only fulfill but *exceed* our expectations, as he did beside the Sea of Galilee (John 6:1-14), is trusting that God the Father actually desires our joy, as Scripture assures us (John 10:10; 1 Peter 4:6; 1 John 4:9).

As our Lord Jesus gives us this line of his prayer, he subtly reminds us, lest we forget, the very first lesson we learned—one rooted in relationship, one rooted in the "our." We are praying "Give *us* this day *our* daily bread." Have you ever noticed the plurality of this request before? You don't pray "give me this day my daily bread," although much of the time our prayer is very

## Jesus provides us with a valuable insight into the heart of God.

"me-focused." No, Jesus provides us with a valuable insight into the heart of God. Once again, Christ is teaching us what it means to be a son or daughter of God. "We ask for *our* bread from *our* Father, because parents produce families, not individuals. . . . We're praying for all of our brothers and sisters' needs too."[17]

Our **reliance** is not only on God. In relying on him, we will also, inevitably, be forced to rely on others, for God works through creation. The Creator uses created things (even us) to fulfill and generously exceed the needs of his creation (John 6:13). So this prayer is not that God would miraculously rain manna in third-world countries or fill the coffers of every soup kitchen from Cleveland to Calcutta. No, the prayer is that God would fulfill our needs, all that we **rely** on him for, *in any way he sees fit,* each and every day. We pray that the Holy Spirit would move in people's hearts to donate and serve. We pray that the Holy Spirit would move in people's hearts to ask for and humbly accept charity from their fellow human beings.

Possibly more than anything else, this request for our daily bread is a request for daily mercy. Our salvation **relies** solely on God's mercy, even after we die and our physical, daily hungers finally cease.

### Our daily dread?

What does this daily **reliance** on God look like? In the American culture, for instance, in which we take such pride in our freedoms and liberties, how do we become dependent on God, as Jesus is encouraging us to do in this line of his prayer? How do we celebrate our independence politically and socially while we seemingly relinquish our independence spiritually?

Our primary **reliance** on God is reflected in our prayer. Little or no prayer life is a commentary on how much we truly do (or do not) **rely** on our heavenly Father. If we have a robust prayer life, it demonstrates a profound **reliance** on God. If your goal is eternal life, your earthly life ought to reflect that goal. If my desire is to be in communion with God forever (in heaven), shouldn't my weekly calendar reflect a desire to be in communion with him while I'm still on earth?

This is God's desire for us: total and complete **reliance** on him daily. Why? Because God knows well that his love is the only love that is eternal and unfailing. God desires that we desire him for our own well-being. Truthfully, then, prayer should be more important to me than oxygen. A lack of oxygen will kill my brain and eventually my body; a lack of prayer will slowly destroy my soul. If I stop breathing, I'll meet Jesus. If I stop praying, who knows who I'll meet?

The Catholic Church is rich in tradition and offers many ways to pray—there is something for everyone. But since we're talking about "daily bread," let's start with how we observe the Lord's Day. What does it mean to "keep holy the Sabbath?" In the minds of many churchgoers, it means not missing Sunday Mass, because doing so is a mortal sin. Indeed, missing Sunday Mass is a mortal sin, but the truth is that the third commandment is far more encompassing than just that hour or so of worship.

In the time of Christ, the Sabbath had far more significance. You could not work on the Sabbath—you could not head to the

> **The Sabbath was a weekly and physical reminder of our need for total reliance on God.**

well to get water, you could not milk your goat, you could not prepare food with any sort of effort, you could not even walk a great distance. The Sabbath was set aside for rest, yes, but also for worship; the Sabbath existed for communion with God and his people. The Sabbath was a weekly and physical reminder of the need for our total **reliance** on God.

Does your Sunday resemble such a prioritization?

One of the reasons we often don't feel that intense "hunger" for the Bread of Life is that our diets are so filled with junk food. Everything that takes our time and attention away from God on Sunday, such as shopping, cleaning, laundry, or yard work, is a synthetic with no nutritional value to our system. Certainly we have a lot to get done around the house and in our families, but how different our lives and relationships would look if we spent a majority of our Sundays praying and playing and less of it catching up on the past week or getting ahead on the week to come.

But we need to pray not just on Sundays but on every day of the week. Even if we can't get to daily Mass, the Church offers us a rhythm to fulfill our daily hunger in the cycle of readings and the Liturgy of the Hours. Christ was raised as a devout Jew and undoubtedly prayed the *Shema* (Scripture verses from the Pentateuch, see Deuteronomy 6:4; 11:13-21; Numbers 15:37-41) morning, noon, and night. He believed in the importance of having regular, regimented, and rhythmic prayer, in communion with God and with fellow believers, as part of his daily life. The Word of God (Scripture) was indispensable to the eternal Word of God (Jesus). With a rhythm such as this, prayer becomes like breathing, and we begin to **rely** on it—and on the God to whom we direct our prayers.

Jesus was teaching and modeling a life of reckless abandon, totally **reliant** on the Father in heaven. Christ himself **relied** on Mary and Joseph. Think about that: The God of the universe in his grand plan of salvation chose to **rely** on the Holy Family for his care, sustenance, protection, and instruction. If for no other

> **Jesus was teaching and modeling a life of reckless abandon, totally reliant on the Father in heaven.**

reason, this fact alone ought to cause all Christians to pause and reflect on the honor they give to the Virgin Mary. We do well in honoring the Blessed Mother—and St. Joseph—for in doing so, we model what God modeled for us. Our prayer ought to be "Lord, help me to **rely** on the only humans you chose to **rely** on so profoundly." This is a prayer in which petition and intercession collide in grace.

## Responding to This Petition

### *Putting Christ in the center of our daily lives*

I was sitting in a chapel once in adoration of the Blessed Sacrament when I noticed that something (or, point in fact, "someone") was missing. I was kneeling probably twenty feet away from the altar. The monstrance, the sacred vessel used to hold the Eucharist, was on the altar. My eyes not being what they once were, I just assumed that Christ was exposed in the monstrance. My tired eyes strained to survey the beautiful gold vessel, only to realize that it was, indeed, empty.

I felt so foolish. Why was I kneeling in front of this empty icon? When Christ's true presence is within it, adoration makes

sense. Without Christ in the center, however, adoration is fruit-
less. Without the Eucharist, I felt as if I were kneeling in front
of a paperweight, albeit an expensive, beautifully handcrafted
paperweight. That's what people might think who don't believe
the Eucharist veils the total and true presence of our Lord Jesus
Christ, body, blood, soul, and divinity. But for those who do, adoration is an incredible and tangible encounter with God's grace.

"Grace" is a funny word to Catholics. As has been said already,
grace is God's life in us. The Greek word for grace is *charis*. You
might recognize it in the word "Eu**charis**t." The Eucharist is one
way that God physically puts his life (grace) into us. What a
stunningly simple yet important reminder of the power of the
sacraments entrusted to our priests! What does it take to forgive
us our sins? Grace. How do we get to heaven? Grace. How do
we get through the day? Grace.

By God's grace he doesn't merely meet our needs; he exceeds
them in the Eucharist. Our **reliance** on him has not only been fulfilled as it was with manna, it has been exceeded by incalculable
proportions. Empowered by the Eucharist, the monstrance of our
body now serves its designed purpose: to offer glory, honor, and
praise to God, not to us. When we are a Eucharistic people—when
we seek the Eucharist, hunger for it, and go frequently to Mass
and adoration—we have Christ literally at the center of our physical lives. We can each fulfill our purpose. When we lose touch
or, more to the point, lose communion with the Eucharist, we
become like the empty monstrance—handcrafted by God, shiny
and beautiful, but empty. Without Christ we are unable to fulfill
the vocation or purpose for which he each of designed us. We are
pleasing to the eyes of the world, but empty in so many ways.

Thus, our **reliance** on him should serve to point others to **rely** on him. God hungers for us to hunger for him. His desire is not to be the weekend date when we're lonely or the rabbit's foot when

> **God hungers for us to hunger for him.**

a difficult phone call comes. He isn't offering us this grace in such a humble, tangible way merely because he desires for us to consume him but because he desires to consume us with his love. If we are authentically thirsty and hungry for God (Isaiah 55:1-3) and trust that he will give us the very best that he has—abundantly (Joshua 5:9-12) and not just enough to survive on—we will have a much easier time **relying** on him each day.

The more we can wrap our heads around the fact that God desires to dwell within us, the more intentional we can be about making our monstrance a worthy dwelling place for God. Of course, to be made a worthy dwelling place might mean we need to look more deeply into ourselves and discover where we need to reconcile with God.

## Questions for Reflection and Discussion

1. Does your prayer life (or lack thereof) demonstrate a true reliance on God or more commonly a "self" reliance, with God there in case of emergencies? Explain.

2. What is your favorite form of prayer, and why?

3. What is your least favorite form of prayer and why?

4. What, if anything, keeps you from getting to Mass more than once a week? What keeps you from reading more Scripture—even daily? What are some concrete things you can do to live more "in rhythm" with the Church?

5. Do you think others would characterize you as "hungry" for God and "reliant" on him? Why or why not?

# CHAPTER TEN

# "Forgive Us Our Trespasses"
# The Intimacy of **RECONCILIATION**

Something happens to a driver when he sees a police car pulling up behind him in his rearview mirror. He begins driving in slow motion. Suddenly the letter of the law (the actual speed limit) is more important than the spirit of the law (a few miles over the speed limit). The leniency we afford ourselves in regard to the law is directly proportional to the proximity of "the law" to our back bumper.

The last time I was pulled over, my three-year-old was in the car with me. "Why are we stopping, Daddy? Were you going speed?" a cute voice inquired from the backseat. "No, sweetie, the nice policeman just wants to talk to Daddy," I replied in a hope-filled response.

The police officer approached my window and pulled off his sunglasses in an exaggerated way, implying a true annoyance with me. "*Do you know why I pulled you over?*" he asked. I hate when they ask that question. They obviously know; they're trained and skilled in the interpretation and enforcement of the law, so why not just tell me what I've done, and let's get on with our respective days.

As he proceeded to give me an unsolicited lesson in traffic safety, I realized that he was not going to have mercy on me. I couldn't get a word in. There would be no opportunity to plead my case or talk my way out of anything. I thought the speed limit was thirty-five miles per hour, and I was going forty. The actual speed limit was thirty. I had broken the law, and I had to suffer the consequences.

My initial response as he walked back to his car with my license and registration to write up the ticket was one of annoyance and anger. "What a jerk!" I silently thought to myself. "Not even a warning, not even the chance to explain my mistake. He's just trying to fill his end-of-the-month quota. That's just wrong."

As I looked in the rearview mirror, my indignation growing and quite evident on my face, I saw not a police car but a look of innocence, virtue, and joy gleefully looking back at me. "What are you smiling about, beautiful girl?" I inquired as I regained perspective on my morning. "I love policemen. We had one come to our school. They keep us safe. We should pray for him," she offered with an authenticity that left me humbled . . . and speechless.

After handing me my ticket, the police officer pulled away in his car. I did not. I sat there for a few minutes, shaking my head in disbelief. How and when had I, a child of God the Father, turned into such a brat? It was no longer about speeding; it was about the attitude of my heart.

### Hide-and-seek

I can justify almost any sin I commit. All it requires is my neck. I need only look to the right and left to find others who are "far worse than I am." That right-to-left maneuver not only allows my soul to take a spring break from sanctity, but it also justifies my selfishness, robs me of my joy, and keeps me trapped in sin.

On the morning of the speeding ticket, I had broken the law, regardless of my ignorance of the true speed limit. I had allowed myself leniency; what *I believed* about the law became my law rather than what the law really stated. That prideful misstep is common in traffic, but deadly in our moral decision making. If

**Our justification of our sin leads to a deadly formula: No sin equals no need for a savior.**

we begin to view our actions through the lens of what *we think is sin* (subjective), we not only lose our consciousness of sin—of right and wrong, life and death—but even worse, we reject God's mercy. We abandon our need for God. Our justification of our sin leads to a deadly formula: No sin equals no need for a savior. As Pope John Paul II once said, "Freedom consists not in doing what we like, but in having the right to do what we ought."

In our modern culture, many have been infected with the thinking that we humans are the gods, so we can decide for ourselves what is right and wrong. Even a cursory glance at the truth God offers us in Scripture reminds us of something we cannot afford to forget: God did not give Adam and Eve the right to decide what was good or evil (subjective truth); God gave Adam and Eve free will, the right *to choose between* good and evil. What was good and what was evil were not up for speculation, debate, discernment, or conjecture, because God loves us too much to allow us to misinterpret such a thing—the consequences are truly eternal.

Adam and Eve bought into the lie of the serpent. Rather than running to God for mercy and asking him to remove the venom of that snakebite, they wallowed in self-pity, playing hide-and-seek with the Creator who had given them everything. They chose sin, and as a result tasted far more than fruit. They (and we) tasted sickness, sadness, pain, and death.

We often do the same. We sin and blame others. We even sin and blame God. Many Catholics get "pulled over" by the Church—called out of their sin—only to respond with clichés: "What does he (the priest) know—he's celibate?" or "The Church needs to get with the times." If only we would remember that it takes a lot less energy to do what's right than to explain why it's not wrong.

We are Adam and Eve, and the problem isn't the "apple"— it's our appetites. We want what we can't have. We believe we're entitled. We forsake everything else to gratify our desires, losing sight of the beauty and perfection we've been freely given. We

## Like Adam and Eve, our first failure is not trusting in God's goodness.

bite into the lie, believing that the One who gave us the life, the breath, the garden, and the blessings to begin with must be holding something back from us. Like Adam and Eve, our first failure is not trusting in God's goodness. Our second failure is failing to take ownership of our sin, which is a lack of trust (again) in his mercy.

Adam and Eve went and hid. We hide too. We may not be hiding under bushes or behind trees, but we play hide-and-seek with God all the time. We hide by not darkening the door of the Church during periods of darkness in our moral life. We hide by disengaging from relationships that hold us accountable. We hide behind excuses of busyness as to why we haven't been to confession. We justify our sins in a thousand ways rather than **reconciling** them with the only One who can actually justify us. We're not as stupid when we commit the sin as we are when we refuse to **reconcile** it with so merciful a God!

Some of us don't believe our sins to be that severe because we judge ourselves by other sinners around us rather than by the God before us and within us. Others of us mistake God's great mercy for weakness, doubting that sin really has any effect on us, now *or later*. Still others of us have gotten so used to justifying our sinfulness that we've lost all sense of reality. Free will isn't a free pass to sin. Just because you *can* do something doesn't mean that you *should* do it. Our eyes have grown so comfortable in the dark that any exposure to the light of Christ makes the eyes of our soul dilate too quickly and painfully.

In this way we especially dislike Mother Church because she, out of love, is the one flipping on the light switch. Ironically, though, it's for this reason that we should love the Church even more. The Church calls us out of our sin and offers us the mercy of God to insure we don't remain dead in sin but alive in Christ. The great Catholic author G. K. Chesterton wrote that the Church "is the only thing that frees a man from the degrading slavery of being a child of his age."[18] He also reminded people that the Church offers more than good counsel or psychotherapy; it offers Christ's absolution.

### Missionary territory

It was the third night of a parish mission I was leading in Florida. I was quite humbled by the invitation, as it was my first experience working with adults in such a setting. I was barely thirty years old, a lay missionary with no experience or résumé. I boarded a plane with little to offer other than the affirming trust of the priest's invitation to lead his flock for three nights of their Lenten journey.

I prayed and prepared. I prayed and studied. I prayed and practiced. The first two nights of the mission went surprisingly well. The third night was supposed to be the "easy" night. The talk was to be shorter, and communal penance was scheduled to follow. I just needed to help people get into the right framework for examining their consciences.

The lights dimmed. A dozen priests vested and took their assigned seats around the perimeter of the church's interior. I shared from my heart. We prayed. Lines formed. People rose as sinners and departed as saints. On the surface nothing miraculous happened. But nothing could have prepared me for what happened next.

"Mark, may I speak with you for a moment?" an elderly gentleman asked. He seemed perplexed and jubilant at the same time. "I don't know where to begin," he said. "I'm Joe. I didn't want to come tonight. I didn't want to come to this thing at all the past three nights. Don't know why I did, to be honest with you—no offense."

"None taken, Joe." I replied with a reassuring smile.

"You see, I've been Catholic all my life. I've never missed Mass, except during the war when we didn't have a priest. But I always hated confession. I always thought, 'What business is it of some priest what I did wrong? He's a sinner just like me. Hell, he's probably worse than me.'"

"I don't know about *him*, Joe, but I bet I am," I said in an effort to lighten the situation. He laughed and nodded.

"It's just that, when you were talking tonight, talking about God being a different kind of Father and Jesus being your Savior and the priest being Jesus' body and all—I had never really thought about it like that before. I wanted what you had, so I went to confession."

At that moment I witnessed a bravery and a freedom in this World War II vet that would have dwarfed even the bravery he had displayed and the freedom he had won on the battlefield. I saw a bravery rooted in virtue and a freedom offered only by God. Tears streamed down his face as he continued. "Before tonight, I hadn't been to confession in forty-six years. When that young priest put his hand on my head and said, 'I absolve you,' I've never felt like that before. I just . . . I can't . . . find the words." At that moment Joe was unable to continue speaking. For a few minutes, God's mercy had rendered both of us speechless. That night, in a suburban Florida parish, a sinner had become a saint, again.

Joe and I prayed together. He told me about his family, many of whom were estranged from him. We spoke of new beginnings, second chances, and the limitless love and mercy of God. He left

> **Three little words that usher in insurmountable graces: "I absolve you."**

that night lighter, and with good reason. Forty six years: that's at least 16,790 sunrises of guilt, shame, brokenness, and pain. All were erased in an instant with just three little words that usher in insurmountable graces: "I absolve you."

Notice the priest does not say, "Jesus absolves you" or even "The Church absolves you." No, it's far deeper, far more mystical and mysterious than that. The priest, sitting *in persona Christi capitas* ("in the person of Christ the head") says, "I absolve you." That first person reminds us of the second Person of the Trinity. The priest is sitting in the person of Christ, offering him his hands and voice and physical presence in that moment of **reconciliation.**

The priest is offering himself to God for service. The sinner is offering himself to God for mercy and grace. This is the encounter that Hebrews 4:14-16 foreshadows when it describes Christ as the great high priest who can sympathize with our weaknesses and to whom we can go for mercy and grace. This intimate gift of self is what the sacraments are all about. We've already discussed the intimacy of the Eucharist. Before we can receive the grace of God in his body and blood, we must come face-to-face with our sin and his grace.

## *The intimacy of reconciliation*

I was not the least bit interested in high school biology and got by with a C. Had I listened to my biology teacher, however, I would have learned many things—among them that cells have short, microscopic hairs called *cilia.* Our eyelashes are also called cilia, and when humans sit eyelash to eyelash, it could be called "ciliation." The Sacrament of Reconciliation is an "eyelash-to-eyelash" encounter with the love and the mercy of God. It is intimate and interpersonal. More than an exchange of words or pleasantries, sorrows, or penitence (though it is that), **reconciliation** is an intimate exchange of death and life. God replaces our death with his life—once again—in the most personal of ways. Although I was a cradle Catholic, this is the intimacy that I had longed for from God all of my life.

## Responding to This Petition

### *Getting right and staying right*

Most of us have a pretty limited view of the Sacrament of Reconciliation. We know that it wipes away our sin, frees us from our debt, and makes us square with God once again. While this is all true, it's not a broad enough perspective because it fails to see God so much at work for our salvation.

Confession doesn't just erase sin; it replaces sin with God's divine life and power. Through the power of the Holy Spirit, acting in the sacramental priesthood, our Lord literally transforms sin into love and death into life. This transformation is nothing less than miraculous. It's also liturgical in the sense that in the same way in which we bring forward bread and wine to be transformed within the Mass, so do we bring forward our guilt, shame, sin, and contrition to be transformed within the confessional. In both cases, whether we bring forward bread and wine or sin and shame, it's God who does the work. We do nothing except present the elements for him to transform into his glory.

> **God's mercy and love flow freely and intentionally, proactively yet unforced.**

A closer examination of Sacred Scripture echoes this truth, that God does the work. God is constantly working for our salvation. The minute the fall occurs in Genesis, he is already promising us a redeemer (3:15). The prodigal Father is already scanning the horizon before the son begins running home (Luke 15:20). The Good Shepherd is already leaving the ninety-nine to find his lost sheep (Luke 15:4). The woman doesn't wait for the coin to turn up; she tears the house apart (Luke 15:8).

God's mercy and love flow freely and intentionally, proactively yet unforced. Just think about the woman at the well, Peter drowning in the sea, the centurion's servant, Jairus' daughter, Peter's mother-in-law, the lepers, the blind man, the woman with the hemorrhage, the demoniacs, the woman caught in adultery, Lazarus in the grave, the high priest's servant in the garden. The list goes on and on.[19]

How long has it been since you've felt the hand of grace upon your head? When was the last time you allowed the words of absolution to remove that Atlas-like weight upon your shoulders?

If your sin feels "too big," then your vision of God is too small. Don't walk. Run. **Reconcile** yourself.

And once you "get right" with God, how do you stay right?

Take an honest look at your life. What relationships lead you away from God? What relationships do not actively help you grow closer to God? What environments, rooms, and locations do you most often find yourself tempted to sin? What times of day and days of the week do you most often sin? What other factors, like hunger, stress, fatigue, or boredom, lead to sin? Are there any addictions, chemicals (like alcohol or drugs), cravings, or struggles that need to be addressed?[20]

These questions are crucial to ask and vital to answer if you really want to turn a corner in your faith life and break the chains of sin. The more honest you can be with yourself, asking God for his grace to help and looking to his Church for answers, the better you will become at protecting this state of grace that you are in. The Act of Contrition is not just a plea for God's grace in avoiding even the near occasions of sin. This prayer is a vital reminder to us for our need to be more proactive and vigilant in protecting our state of grace.

If we really are grateful for the mercy and grace available to us in the Sacrament of Reconciliation, we will undoubtedly want to share our joy with all whom we encounter. We will want them to taste a similar freedom from God and, if necessary, from us.

## Questions for Reflection and Discussion

1. Do you most often judge your holiness by comparing yourself to the people around you or by comparing yourself to Christ? Explain.

2. Do you look forward to the Sacrament of Reconciliation, loathe going, or neither? Explain.

3. Is this understanding of "reconciliation" as a face-to-face, eyelash-to-eyelash encounter with Jesus Christ himself new to you? Do you experience a deep, intimate connection with Christ during this sacrament? Why or why not?

4. In the "Responding to This Petition" section, did any one sentence—either a visual image, an assertion, or a question— comfort, convict, or afflict you? Explain.

5. When is the next time you can get to Sacrament of Reconciliation? Are you willing to tell someone else when you are going so that he or she can hold you accountable?

CHAPTER ELEVEN

# "As We Forgive Those Who Trespass against Us" The Need for **REPENTANCE**

I t's difficult to separate the last chapter from this one, as the line "Forgive us our trespasses as we forgive those who trespass against us" really is one piece. But St. Luke is no stranger to giving us the whole story in two parts. His story of the prodigal son has two parts as well.

### When we last left our heroes . . .

In a previous chapter, we discussed the first half of the prodigal parable. The prodigal father had just welcomed home his young son (Luke 15:20-24). It's a scene that great films are made of, as the penitent son rushes home into the arms of his forgiving father. Imagine the perfect sunset, Oscar-winning music, and flashbacks to the boy's childhood, all in slow motion.

But if I were the director, it's at this moment that I'd set the stage for a sequel. You'd hear the lively music beginning to play. You'd see the party starting as the reunited father and son, arms locked around one another's shoulders, begin their walk back to the estate. Then the camera would slowly pan off the prodigal pair to reveal a forgotten older brother. His face would be filled with vengeance—teeth clenched, lips pursed, and eyes hard and cold. The look would foreshadow—and insure—the success of the next film.

How often do you think about the older brother in the prodigal parable? Most homilies focus on the younger son's relationship to the father (and rightly so), but few unpack the relationship of the older brother in this most famous parable. What of the one who did the right thing? What went through *his heart* that night of the homecoming party?

### It's not my party

The news of his younger brother's homecoming must have infuriated this older brother. He would have watched the servants rushing around in preparation for the great feast, and the fatted calf being escorted out of its holding pen. Dead tired and covered in dirt from an honest day's work, he would have seen this no-good brother, now robed and slipper-clad, sitting as the guest of honor.

The playboy was back, and the plowboy wasn't happy.

"Your brother was dead and has come back to life," the father explained to him. But he had grown fond of being the "good son." What was he feeling now? Was it jealousy at the attention showered on his younger sibling? Was it how quickly his father had forgotten who'd remained loyal and steadfast? Was it how prodigal and wasteful the father had appeared to be, first with his inheritance and now with the robe, the ring, the calf, and the party?

Everything the father had was also his, the father reminded the older brother. He had not been cheated. He wasn't going to starve or be forced to live without. But the older brother's goal was not the same as the father's. The older brother wanted justice in the eyes of the world; the father was offering justice in the eyes of heaven. The father offered unconditional love with the hope that his older son was like him in more ways than his work ethic.

The older brother was making a critical tactical error. He had the sense that he deserved his father's wealth and admiration. His attitude was one of expectation and entitlement. In holding a grudge, he was betraying not only his brother but also his father, who was offering mercy to the returning brother. The older son was in no way acting like his father; pouting, he wouldn't even join the celebration (Luke 15:28).

What can we take from this episode? In the Lord's Prayer, Christ is not only giving us a glimpse into the Father's heart but demonstrating the prayer by which we can become more like God, made more perfectly into his image. The prayer reveals how we can become one with God's will as Christ is one with the Father. Jesus is showing us that to become like God, we can't just stop

> **We need to repent of our smallness and seek God's greatness.**

at having our sins forgiven. We must *offer forgiveness* and mercy to all of our brothers and sisters. "To err is human, to forgive is divine. When we forgive, we act as God acts."[21]

Our entire way of thinking needs to change. We need a heart transplant. We need to **repent** of our smallness and seek God's greatness.

### Sin relents when a sinner repents

Several years ago on Ash Wednesday, I dutifully went forward to receive ashes. I quickly became demoralized in line as I saw those ahead of me retreating back to their chairs with what looked like a gallon of black paint smeared across their brows. The deacon whose line I had inadvertently ended up in was taking his ash-allocation duties to glorious new heights. I slowly crept forward, praying he would feel less enthused when it came time to deface my forehead.

The moment I actually received my ashes seemed to take forever. The deacon was very intentional in his words. He didn't offer the "ashes to ashes, dust to dust" formula that I had become so accustomed to while growing up. No, he offered the more modern prayer based on Mark 1:15, saying, "Turn away from sin, and return to the gospel." Something happened in my heart at that moment. It was as though my soul were a xylophone and each word a mallet. The deacon had struck a chord while giving me those ashes, and I retreated back to the pew, very humbled, a little dazed, and quite confused.

It was in that moment that everything collided—ritual, tradition, Scripture, sin, grace, pride, humility—and it felt as though God had just turned me inside out. I bore the mark of a penitent

## Would I just wear the ashes or actually engage in what they signified?

sinner on my exterior, but what of my interior? The choice was now mine. Would I just wear the ashes or actually engage in what they signified? Would I sleepwalk through the ritual or run forward into authentic **repentance**?

I reflected on the two commands in the Scripture verse the deacon had shared. **Repentance** has two distinct movements of the heart. First, we are to "turn away from sin." Imagine yourself standing in a doorway. You are peering into a dark room, with no hint of light anywhere. Behind you is bright light, but your body is turned away so not even your peripheral vision can detect it. You can feel the warmth and sense the brightness behind you, but your eyes are locked on the darkness before you.

The first action of **repentance**, the "turning away from sin," is a ninety-degree movement to the right. You are no longer trapped by sin. Your gaze unlocked from its tantalizing clutches, you are now faced with an equally difficult task. Merely turning ninety degrees has left you "better off" but not free. There is still the risk of duplicity. There is still darkness calling you to slavery as the light beckons you to freedom. Sadly, this was often the position I chose to stand in. I liked the availability of the light as it warmed my soul. I enjoyed the selfish depravity of the darkness, too, as it enveloped my flesh. I was trapped in the mire of a lukewarm existence, unwilling to abandon myself to the light.

Fortunately, God was unwilling to abandon me to the darkness. He kept calling out to me, offering me freedom. I knew well the bad news of sin. The gospel was offering me the good news of God's salvation. It's in the next ninety degrees that we fully comprehend **repentance**. The second action is a "returning to the gospel." It's in this movement that we forsake the lies and the false securities of the sin and turn completely away from the darkness. It's in this movement that we face God's magnificent light with our whole existence.

Now, this full 180-degree movement of **repentance** is not easy. For many of us, it might feel like a spiritual tennis match, back and forth, from darkness to light, every day of our lives. This is one of the reasons that our Church takes an entire season to focus on **repentance** and not just one week. Think about it. The Church could say we're going to take one week to prepare our hearts for Easter, but would we really be prepared? If we are dead from sin, would one week be enough of a jolt to our spiritual system to get our hearts pumping and blood flowing in the right direction again? Even if it were enough, making a 180-degree turn in our lifestyles in one week—going from the dark to the light that quickly—would blind us. No, the Church in her wisdom takes us by the hand as Saul's companions did (Acts 9:8) or as the friends of the paralytic (Luke 5:18), walking us to our destination slowly and methodically, to insure that our systems can handle our imminent healing and bold new life.

What we often lose sight of in the process of **repentance** is the "our" that we spoke of earlier. We are united by and in the body of Christ. Our sins are not private. Even those sins we might blindly believe have no effect or bearing on anyone else, even those sins affect our ability to love and to receive love properly. Sin is cancerous, much more deadly than secondhand smoke.

In our returning to the gospel, we are also returning to the community, hat in hand, seeking their forgiveness as well. That's one of the reasons (by no means the only one) that we go to a

> **When we sin against our brothers, we sin against Christ himself.**

priest for the Sacrament of Reconciliation. We are acknowledging to the priest, who is standing in for the community, that our personal sin has strained our relationship to the greater body.

In doing this, we fulfill our baptismal promises to live a new life in Christ, *as long as* we are willing to seek *and offer* forgiveness to anyone we have been hurt by or sinned against. When we sin against our brothers, we sin against Christ himself. This is the depth of **repentance,** as well as the challenge of it. When we sin against God, we sin against our own family.

Why is it so difficult for us to put our own wants and needs and comfort second and to put others first? Why is this 180-degree shift of **repentance** on our part—away from self and back to God in others—so difficult? Many would say that putting ourselves second is stupid. "You got to look out for number one."

Christ knew people might say that.

### The unforgiving servant . . . is me

The apostles frequently asked Jesus questions. Let's revisit one scene in particular, in which Simon Peter the fisherman comes to the Savior with a math problem.

> Then Peter came up and said to him, "Lord, how often shall my brother sin against me, and I forgive him? As many as seven times?" Jesus said to him, "I do not say to you seven times, but seventy times seven." (Matthew 18:21-22)

Oh, poor Peter, always willing to open mouth and insert sandal. It wasn't really his fault; it's the human condition. When we've been wronged, we believe in turning the other cheek . . . once, maybe twice, but what about being made the fool? Every time we get wronged, our body instinctively begins to retreat. God doesn't want us to be taken advantage of, right?

We are not unlike Peter. We should be thankful to him; he's the guy in class who asks the question we're afraid to ask—and then gets chastised for asking it. Jesus is obviously not putting a limit on forgiveness. "Seventy times seven" is meant to evoke the idea of limitlessness. Peter was looking for the letter of the law; Jesus was giving the spirit of it. Why do we insist on putting limits on how much we should (or should not) forgive others? Jesus answers Peter's question with the following parable:

"Therefore the kingdom of heaven may be compared to a king who wished to settle accounts with his servants. When he began the reckoning, one was brought to him who owed him ten thousand talents; and as he could not pay, his lord ordered him to be sold, with his wife and children and all that he had, and payment to be made. So the servant fell on his knees, imploring him, 'Lord, have patience with me, and I will pay you everything.' And out of pity for him the lord of that servant released him and forgave him the debt. But that same servant, as he went out, came upon one of his fellow servants who owed him a hundred denarii; and seizing him by the throat he said, 'Pay what you owe.' So his fellow servant fell down and pleaded with him, 'Have patience with me, and I will pay you.' He refused and went and put him in prison till he should pay the debt. When his fellow servants saw what had taken place, they were greatly distressed, and they went and reported to their lord all that had taken place. Then his lord summoned him and said to him, 'You wicked servant! I forgave you all that debt because you pleaded with me; and should not you have had mercy on your fellow servant, as I had mercy on you?' And in anger his lord delivered him to the jailers, till he should pay all his debt. So also my heavenly Father will do to every one of you, if you do not *forgive your brother from your heart*." (Matthew 18:23-35; emphasis added)

There is much that is happening in this episode, far too much to offer an exegetical study here. On a fundamental level, however, this parable is less a commentary on the justice and charity of the master (God) and more about the lack of charity or justice on the part of the servant (you and me). The master "did a 180"; the servant did not. Now the master wanted to insure some **repentance** on the part of the one whom he had so graciously forgiven.

Notice *how* you are to forgive your brother. How does the stipulation "from your heart" change the commandment? As a child, did you ever say "Sorry" for hitting your sibling because

## Forgiving of others is a movement motivated by authentic repentance.

Mom or Dad made you do it (but you really had no sorrow for the action)? This forgiveness goes far deeper than words. This forgiveness must be authentic and rooted in humility. Refusing to forgive someone else is equivalent to refusing God's mercy toward yourself. Forgiving of others is a movement motivated by authentic **repentance**.

We need to **repent** for our lack of mercy toward others. When it comes to forgiveness, do you hold others to a higher standard than you hold yourself? Do you get angry when other people "don't listen to you" as you, in turn, refuse to listen to them? Have you ever desired forgiveness without being willing to forgive someone against whom you hold a grudge?

It's so interesting that Peter is the one who asks Jesus the initial question. No other apostle is listed by name in this passage. It is significant, as Peter is the one so desperately seeking forgiveness from our Lord following his passion. It's in that moment that Christ gives Peter a crash course in mercy. Jesus' answers demonstrate that Peter's **repentance** to God is indissolubly linked to the charity and mercy he, in turn, shows to the greater body of Christ. Remember their breakfast following the resurrection, the one with the three questions? Jesus asks Peter, "Do you love me?" When Peter says that he does, Jesus responds: "Feed my sheep" (John 21:15-17).

### What did Jesus do?

God isn't one of those "Do as I say, not as I do" kind of people. The incarnation is the prime example of God saying "Do as I do." When Christ emptied himself and took flesh, God literally became what he desires; Jesus is the living example by which we will be measured. He went forward to be baptized, though he was without sin. He did this out of loving example for us. The same way in which the River Jordan marked the climactic end to a journey of exile for the Israelites, Christ's baptism in the Jordan revealed the path to a new freedom from the exile of sin into the promised land of God's grace.

Through Christ, God the Father wasn't only offering forgiveness to his children but also to his brothers and sisters—every imaginable type of character in creation—at every turn. Consider the last few hours of Jesus' life on Good Friday. Ponder how freely he offered *forgiveness to those who had trespassed against the body*, his and ours.

In the praetorium, Pilate offered the crowd a choice between Barabbas and Jesus (Matthew 27:15-17). Barabbas knew his sins. There was no sign of **repentance** or remorse, yet Christ took his sins upon himself. Interestingly, the name Barabbas comes from two words: "bar" meaning "son of" and "Abba" meaning "Father." Christ the Son took the place of "the Father's son"; he took my place and he took your place.

How about those jeering and mocking him in his weakest physical moments (Luke 23:35-39)? As the Living Water hung there thirsty, as the Transfigured One was disfigured, how did they respond? They didn't believe themselves wrong; they didn't **repent**. They mocked Mercy. Still, they received mercy in return.

What of "the good thief" that tradition calls Dismas? Guilty of his crimes, he "got what he deserved" in the eyes of the people. Unlike Barabbas, this didn't seem to be Dismas' lucky day. My, how things changed as he peered into the eyes of mercy! Dismas went to confession on his cross (Luke 23:40-43). No screen necessary, no kneeler available. This son of the Father came running home with tears in his eyes and found not only a loving Father's embrace but his older brother as well, waiting with open arms on the adjacent cross. His **repentance** sincere, he tasted mercy, and his worst day became his best. His last day became his first—in paradise.

Throughout these scenes we're reminded of the courage and humility it takes both to offer forgiveness and to seek it. **Repentance** doesn't just require humility; it requires courage. These events in Jesus' life remind us that mercy requires strength;

it is not a sign of weakness. This truth is the same for our own lives. Mercy requires fortitude. It's what the older prodigal brother

> **Repentance doesn't just require humility; it requires courage.**

lacked. In fact it's what many "good Catholics" lack (at least two weekends a year, when the "Chreaster" or Christmas/Easter Catholics come home to the Father for a holiday Mass).

## Responding to This Petition

Commit the following verses to memory. They come from St. Matthew's Gospel, immediately before the Lord's Prayer:

> "But I say to you, Love your enemies and pray for those who persecute you, so that you may be sons of your Father who is in heaven; for he makes his sun rise on the evil and on the good, and sends rain on the just and on the unjust. For if you love those who love you, what reward have you?" (Matthew 5:44-46)

Did you catch what Jesus said here? This is the kind of teaching moment that should cause us all to pause, reflect, and (most likely) repent. We aren't measured by how well we love those who love us. We are measured by how well we love those who don't love us. True and perfect love is difficult, not easy.

Do we offer love to those family members who have serious issues with the Church and let it be known every chance they get? Do we seek forgiveness from those with whom we've shared God's truth but in less-than-loving ways? Do we offer forgiveness

> **We are measured by how well we love those who don't love us.**

to those who (for whatever reason) are blind to God's truth or deaf to his voice in their own lives? They need mercy from us, not condemnation. It's easy to fall into the trap of condemning others unless we realize that it is a trap. If we claim to be Christian, we must realize what this means.

It means that our idea of "justice" and "what's fair" might not be God's. Wasn't it God's idea to pay the one-hour workers the same as the full-day workers (Matthew 20:1-16)? It means that when Christ, the Good Shepherd, calls those "sheep" who are far from him (Matthew 18:12), it isn't necessarily the ones "far from your parish" or from the Church. Those most in need of God's mercy might be sitting in the front pew, whose *hearts* are far away, even though their bodies are near him. We need to maintain a posture of **repentance** and joyful love of the sinner, without supporting or condoning the sin.

God's forgiveness knows no limits. God's love is not fickle; Christ loves the pope as much as the prostitute working a corner in Rome just a few miles away. Christ loves the person performing the abortion as much as the person protesting it. Now, that's not to imply that God doesn't care about the sins of others or that their sins do not destroy the body of Christ or the sanctity of life.

It is to remind us that God's love is unconditional, and his mercy, if sought through **repentance**, is freely given *to anyone*.

Pray with humility (the way we always ought to), and remember that you are the only sinner whose behavior you can control. This is the heart of **repentance**. This is the essence of this petition in the Lord's Prayer. How far we are from God is rarely about physical distance but about spiritual openness. And we need that spiritual openness to stay close to the Lord in times of temptation.

## Questions for Reflection and Discussion

1. Which character in the parable of the prodigal son do you identify with the most: the younger (returning) brother, the father, or the older (indignant) brother?

2. Are there any people in your life you have struggled (or are currently struggling) to forgive? If you feel comfortable sharing about it, discuss why you have found it difficult.

3. Has your life been more an existence of being trapped in the darkness, immersed in the light, or standing in between, with one foot in both camps? Explain.

4. Have you ever bought into the devil's lie that your sins are too awful to forgive or that you are too much a disappointment for God to unconditionally love? If not, how do you avoid it? If so, how did you conquer that fear, if you have? Discuss.

# CHAPTER TWELVE

# "Lead Us Not into Temptation"
## Living in **REALITY**

It's important to briefly pause and clarify the meaning of this line of the Lord's Prayer, because it is often the most misunderstood. Many mistakenly believe "Lead us not into temptation" to be a plea to God not to tempt them. To be clear, God does not tempt us to sin, in any way, at any time. Temptation is contrary to God's nature—he is perfect love. A God who loves us would never set us up to fail like that. God wants us to succeed, which is why he gives us so many gifts and aids along the way.

One of God's greatest gifts in the past two decades is the *Catechism of the Catholic Church,* since it gives Catholics concise explanations of some of the most difficult or debated teachings of the Church. Regarding this line from the Lord's Prayer, the *Catechism* reminds us that the Greek means both "do not allow us to enter into temptation" and "do not let us yield to temptation" (2846; Matthew 26:41). So we see that this petition is not a plea to an untrustworthy God playing a cosmic game of cat and mouse with us. Rather, this line reflects a heartfelt plea for mercy and protection. We ask the Father who loves us more than we love ourselves to help us stand strong in the face of life's sinful **realities.**

The truth is that there is an ongoing battle for souls. At this very moment, heaven and hell are waging a war for your soul. Whether you see it depends on whether you have the eyes to see it (see Matthew 13:16). The question for all of us is whether we hide our heads in the sands of life or turn and face **reality**.

### Felt banners are not reality

I was sixteen years old and had the world figured out. I sat in the pew each Sunday, disengaged from the liturgy transpiring before my young, cynical eyes. If my thoughts had been broadcast, those sitting around me (who seemed equally disengaged) would have heard questions like these: Is it your plan to bore me to death, Lord? Could this priest's train of thought derail any more? Does this music make anyone else embarrassed to be Catholic? Do they really think those felt banners look good?

Put charitably, the Church seemed irrelevant to my life and completely out of touch. How could such an institution have anything valid or worthwhile to say about my life? Every week was the same "song and dance." Each Sunday was the same message with different words: "Be nice, and everything will work out." My adolescent body fought off sleep in the pews. The closing song could not come soon enough.

It seemed the Church and I would never find common ground. Heaven was in the clouds, but I was stuck on earth. The Church was living in a fantasy land, but I was steeped in **reality**. I believed the Church to be embroiled in a conspiracy to woo and retain members. If they got me to believe that following Jesus meant that all my problems would melt away, then they'd have me. Well, I wasn't buying it, and for that matter, I wasn't buying the Church.

I wanted a God who spoke to my **reality**. I wanted a God who didn't pretend everything was great when we both knew that it wasn't. I wanted a raw honesty from someone in the Church, and if that wasn't possible, then that Church wasn't for me.

Not long after, I came across a verse that changed my life—forever. The Holy Spirit grants us an invaluable insight through

## I wanted a God who spoke to my reality.

the pen of St. John, and this passage took all of my cynicism and upended it. Jesus is telling his disciples of the suffering he is about to endure. "The hour is coming, indeed it has come, when you will be scattered, every man to his home" (John 16:32). Then he says:

> "I have said this to you, that in me you may have peace. In the world you have tribulation; but be of good cheer, I have overcome the world." (John 16:33)

Jesus didn't just promise his apostles that their lives would be difficult if they *stopped following him*. Jesus promised his followers that their lives would be laced with pain and suffering *even when they followed him*. What is even more poignant was that it was a promise to the disciples that Jesus delivered on the way to his death, at his last meal.

This verse possessed the raw honesty I had been searching for. Christ's message was so clear and his point so paradoxical that it had to be true. Otherwise, what leader in his right mind would say such a thing to his followers? That is not the kind of line you build a marketing campaign around. One has to think that at this moment, some of the apostles were left scratching their heads. I can almost hear Bartholomew or Jude Thaddeus saying under his breath, "Excuse me, Rabbi, what are you talking about? Was that in the fine print? That wasn't part of the bargain when I left my job to go on tour with you!"

Read that verse again. Within the warning about tribulation is also a promise brimming with hope. Jesus promises us that he has overcome the world. Storms will come, yes, but no storm that can wash away his mercy; his mercy washes away our sin. Christ's cross brings meaning—redemptive purpose—to our sufferings. He doesn't promise to shield us from all of life's storms, but he does promise to shelter us within them.

As I sat in that church pew, I felt like a fool. How could I have been so smug and so blind as to think I knew better than all those who had come before me? The Church had no conspiracy theory. The boredom I experienced in liturgy was not because the Church was closeminded, but because I was hard-hearted. I thought I knew the answer before I had asked the right question.

The Church hadn't failed to adapt to the **reality** of the world because it was blind to it; the Church had stood firm in virtue and in truth because the **reality** of the world is not God's reality at all. The **reality** of the situation is that evil is very much alive and that the devil is constantly and subtly skewing our vision to leave us in a state of distrust—distrust of God, distrust of our fellow man, distrust of Christ's Church. No, the Church isn't blind to the **realities** of sin; the Church is more impressed with the sin-vanquishing power of Christ's grace, available in the sacraments.

## *Taking God at his word*

Christ promised us that we would have troubles in life. Ironically, that warning ought to bring us peace. He was warning his followers (then and now) that suffering doesn't necessarily mean that we're doing something wrong. Sometimes it means that we are doing something right. In fact, in the verse immediately prior to this important warning (John 16:32), Christ reminds us that he (and we) are never alone in our trials, because *the Father* is with us; and "if God is for us, who is against us?" (Romans 8:31).

We spoke earlier about the need to trust God as a Father who genuinely wants good things for his children (Matthew 7:7-11) and who wants us to have joy and abundant life (John 10:10). St. Paul, who understood well the lures and temptations of the world, also reminded us that God will always provide for us a way out if we call upon him:

> No temptation has overtaken you that is not common to man. God is faithful, and he will not let you be tempted beyond your strength, but with the temptation will also provide the way of escape, that you may be able to endure it. (1 Corinthians 10:13)

God isn't saying that situations aren't tempting. He knows better than we do the methods and strategies of the devil. St. Angela Merici reminds us that "the devil doesn't sleep but seeks the ruin of our souls in a thousand ways." What God is saying through St. Paul is that *if we have the presence of mind and humility of heart to call upon him*, we can withstand any temptation that comes our way. The truth is that God thinks more of you than you think of yourself.

The first step in truly conquering temptation is to discern where it comes from. If we feel that we are at an impasse or that we are

> ## The truth is that God thinks more of you than you think of yourself.

standing at the moral "fork in the road," we ought to pray before we take another step. We must constantly discern situations that confront us, whether they are trials from God or temptations from the evil one. As already stated, temptations do not come from God. "God cannot be tempted with evil and he himself tempts no one" (James 1:13). God wants to set us free from temptation. He is standing at the juncture where the two roads diverge, pointing us down the often rocky, challenging path that leads to heaven, not the wide and easy path that leads to hell.

God does allow us to be tried and tested so as to refine us and help us grow in virtue. Read more about the differences between trials and temptations on your own, asking the Lord to grant you wisdom to tell the difference: 1 Corinthians 10:13; James 1:12-16; Mark 7:15, 21-23; 1 Timothy 6:9; James 1:2-4, 1:13; Proverbs 1:10-14; Matthew 6:13; Titus 2:11-12; Hebrews 2:18; Romans 8:18.

The same Holy Spirit who inspired these words of Scripture is the One who "makes us *discern* between trials, which are necessary for the growth of the inner man, and temptation, which leads to sin and death" (*Catechism of the Catholic Church*, 2847). The *Catechism* further explains how discernment helps us to see the temptation for what it really is; it "unmasks the lie," revealing that the object that "appears to be good" is "in **reality** . . . death."

Temptations are often not only seductive but subtle. In order to accurately discern the source or situation, prayer is a necessity. Prayer helps us move beyond sin as a word or concept and reveals the truth behind the lies. Prayer exposes the **reality** of life and sifts

> **Temptations are often not only seductive but subtle.**

through all the games we play—when we decide to ignore the red flags, when we reduce sin to lame excuses and justifications, when we continually thrust ourselves into sinful environments and situations and presume that we'll escape unscathed. When we do these things, we are not living in **reality**; we are playing into the hands of the evil one. The Church, too, helps us to see not only the severity of sins (mortal and venial) but also their source. If we want to succeed in the face of temptation, we need to understand the forces at work around and within us.

## Responding to This Petition

### Discerning the tug of war

The word "discern" comes from a Latin term meaning "to separate apart." When we spiritually discern a situation or temptation, we break it down into different parts—its motivations, sources, potential outcomes, and possibilities for good and bad.

Discernment reveals how grace and sin are at work, and how the situation either leads us closer to God or further away from him. There is no third option, for indifference also leads us down the devil's path, just at a slower pace. "Lukewarmness is the devil in disguise."[22] As St. John reminds us, lukewarmness makes God sick to his stomach (Revelation 3:16).

The more we go to the Holy Spirit, asking him for a heightened awareness of our own sinful inclinations, the more focused and sharpened our discernment of temptations become. The Spirit illuminates our minds and hearts (*Catechism of the Catholic Church*, 2670), revealing to us those areas of our lives in which we are allowing our flesh to lead our spirits. St. Paul offers us a beautiful passage on this war between body and soul in his letter to the Romans:

> I do not understand my own actions. For I do not do what I want, but I do the very thing I hate. Now if I do what I do not want, I agree that the law is good. So then it is no longer I that do it, but sin which dwells within me. For I know that nothing good dwells within me, that is, in my flesh. I can will what is right, but I cannot do it. For I do not do the good I want, but the evil I do not want is what I do. Now if I do what I do not want, it is no longer I that do it, but sin which dwells within me.
>
> So I find it to be a law that when I want to do right, evil lies close at hand. (Romans 7:15-21)

Can you relate to this situation within yourself? Do you feel an epic tug-of-war between your body and your soul? Do you feel an angel on one shoulder, calling you on to righteousness, imploring you to virtue? Do you feel the devil (a fallen angel) on your other shoulder, whispering an enticing invitation for you to vice and selfishness? This tug-of-war rages throughout our day.

The devil's tactics and tools are obvious to a discerning heart, but subtle to a worldly one. The Internet, for example, which can be used for much good, also has the potential to lead people into pornography addictions. Beer can be a great accompaniment to a meal, but too much can lead to obesity and alcoholism. Our relationships may look peaceful on the surface, but we may be struggling with unresolved anger and unforgiveness. Temptation becomes the tool necessary for the momentum to shift and for our flesh to lead our soul in places it's not designed to go. "Our soul is too noble to be satisfied with external goods. It is immortal and demands immortal happiness."[23]

So in this petition, we are acknowledging the **reality** of evil. But even more, we are relying on the Holy Spirit's eternal presence to guide and protect us along each step of our daily faith walk. It is when our souls (led by the Spirit) lead our bodies through the tempting **realities** of life that we shatter the chains of cultural slavery.

So then, brethren, we are debtors, not to the flesh, to live according to the flesh—for if you live according to the flesh you will die, but if by the Spirit you put to death the deeds of the body you will live. For all who are led by the Spirit of God are sons of God. For you did not receive the spirit of slavery to fall back into fear, but you have received the spirit of sonship. When we cry, "Abba! Father!" it is the

Spirit himself bearing witness with our spirit that we are children of God. (Romans 8:12-16)

We have learned that God is not the source of our temptations and that we must rely on the Holy Spirit to help us discern the tactics of the evil one and allow the Spirit to guide us along the narrow path to heaven. Now let's discover how the Lord delivers us from this evil that looms before us and challenges us each step of the way.

## Questions for Reflection and Discussion

1. How does the verse from St. John's Gospel (16:33) encouraging peace in the face of persecution leave you feeling about your daily faith walk? Does it offer you peace or pause? Explain.

2. Share a personal story of a time that God's presence and strength helped you survive and conquer fear or temptation.

3. What are some of the tools (obvious or subtle) that you see the devil most frequently using to tempt and ensnare this modern generation? What effects (if any) do these tools have on your family and your faith life?

4. In times of temptation, do you most often cry out to the Father ("Abba") or go at it alone? Explain.

# CHAPTER THIRTEEN

# "Deliver Us from Evil"
# The Children in Need of a **RESCUE**

In the last chapter, we ended by pointing out some of the many tools Satan uses to enslave us so that we would relinquish our freedom and be controlled by created things. When evil enters the story in Genesis, Satan does just that. He tempts us through our pride. He casts doubt on the Father's love. He offers us "control" over creation.

Isn't it sadly ironic that creation would be lured so easily through created things—things created to reflect the love of their Creator—to doubt the love of that same Creator? How often do the things of the created world steal my heart and divert my eyes from the One who created them? How often is God, the Creator, taken out of the equation by the world? He's the lifeguard, trying to **rescue** us at every turn, but we don't even realize that we're drowning.

All angels have a ministry. The devil, too, being an angel (fallen, but an angel nonetheless) has a ministry. The devil's ministry is one of distraction. You'll note that the devil and his demons do not deny God's existence in Scripture; they even proclaim Jesus' identity clearly and plainly (Matthew 4:3-10; Matthew 8:29; Luke 4:33-34). The devil's time isn't spent trying to convince us that God doesn't exist but rather that we cannot trust God. That was the original lie, the first lie breathed into paradise (Genesis 3:1-7).

The devil wants us to believe that God is withholding something from us. If God is "holding back," then he must not be trustworthy, right? If God isn't trustworthy, then all of his promises are empty. If the evil one can fabricate a proverbial "chink in the armor"—even to the slightest degree within our subconscious—he can skillfully, systematically, and subtly exploit that crack of mistrust, every minute of every day of our lives.

Consider now the importance of Christ's teaching us to pray "Deliver us from evil." Jesus is trying to **rescue** us from misguided thinking. He knows well the realities of temptation. Jesus endured

> **Jesus is trying to rescue us from misguided thinking.**

temptation far more insidious and difficult during his journey into the desert than any of us will ever have to endure (Matthew 4:1-11; Luke 4:1-13). It's for this reason that we can feel confident and take God at his word. God has faced temptation, every bit as bad and far worse than ours, and conquered it. How thankful we should be that our God loves us enough to take on flesh and face the temptations of mortal men! How wise we would be to actually take him up on his invitation for help:

> Since then we have a great high priest who has passed through the heavens, Jesus, the Son of God, let us hold fast our confession. For we have not a high priest who is unable to sympathize with our weaknesses, but one who in every

respect has been tempted as we are, yet without sinning. Let us then with confidence draw near to the throne of grace, that we many receive mercy and find grace to help in time of need. (Hebrews 4:14-16)

This is the invitation to be **rescued** from ourselves. We can never forget that Jesus and the devil are not equals. Jesus is the eternal Son of God, the second Person of the Trinity; Jesus Christ is God himself. The devil is merely an angel, and for this reason, God assigns each of us an angel of our own, to aid us on our journey.

### *Angel of God*

Picture an angel in your mind.

You saw two wings and a halo, right? Perhaps a white robe? Where does that mental picture come from? Maybe from a painting you've seen, or possibly a movie. Do you know that Scripture doesn't always depict an angel as having two wings? We see six-winged and four-winged angels more than angels with just two (Isaiah 6:2, 6; Ezekiel 1:6; Revelation 4:8). We see angels adorned in white and in light, but truthfully, our perception of angels comes more from the depictions we've seen than from the word of God.

Sometimes it helps to go back to the primary source to get a more accurate picture of what angels are, what they do, and the purposes they serve. To be clear, angels and guardian angels exist. In fact, the Church even celebrates the guardian angels with their very own feast day on October 2. Scripture affirms their presence:

"Behold, I send an angel before you, to guard you on the way and to bring you to the place which I have prepared. Give heed to him and hearken to his voice, do not rebel against him, for he will not pardon your transgression; for my name is in him." (Exodus 23:20-21)

For he will give his angels charge of you / to guard you in all your ways. / On their hands they will bear you up, / lest you dash your foot against a stone. (Psalm 91:11–12)

If you'd like to read more about our heavenly aides, check out Genesis 22:11-12; Genesis 24:7, 40; Acts 12:5-8, 11, 15; Psalm 34:7; Matthew 4:11; Acts 5:17-20; Acts 8:26; and the *Catechism of the Catholic Church*, 328–54.

Too often we think of angels, who are heavenly bodies, in earthly, bodily terms. They are not human, however, and, therefore not bound by human constraints. They exist to do the will of God, to be his messengers, guides, and defenders—of us and of truth. It's important, though, to remember that they are not to be worshipped (Revelation 19:10; 22:9); they exist for the sole purpose of praising God and carrying out his will. Angels have played significant roles in God's plan of salvation. Think about it:

- An angel stopped Abraham before he killed his son, Isaac (Genesis 22:12).
- An angel "passed over" Egypt, allowing for Moses and the Jews to escape (Exodus 12:11-27).
- An angel announced God's hope and plan to the Virgin Mary (Luke 1:26-38).

- An angel calmed Joseph's fears about taking Mary as his wife (Matthew 1:18-25).
- An angel was at the empty tomb, announcing Jesus' resurrection (Matthew 28:2-7).
- An angel, St. Michael, and his army are waging war for your soul (Revelation 12:7-9).

What do all of these instances have in common? God used his angels to aid in the **rescue** of his children. Angels are alive and at work in our lives. They are one way that God works to deliver

## Angels are an integral part of God's rescue efforts.

us from the works and tactics of the devil. Angels are an integral part of God's **rescue** efforts, a primary way in which he is constantly delivering us from evil. Angels proclaim the greatness of God, echoing the good news of salvation in the heavens and throughout the earth.

### God's rescue mission

Remember that star I spoke about earlier—the one that signaled the fulfillment of the prophecies, the birth of the Messiah? Do you remember what happened after the Magi arrived at King Herod's palace? Herod, a sinister and wicked man, had secretly summoned the Wise Men to ascertain the exact time the star had appeared (Matthew 2:7). Under the guise of his own desire to worship Jesus, he instructed the Magi to return and report Christ's location. Then God intervened.

And being warned in a dream not to return to Herod, they departed to their own country by another way.

Now when they had departed, behold, an angel of the Lord appeared to Joseph in a dream and said, "Rise, take the child and his mother, and flee to Egypt, and remain there till I tell you; for Herod is about to search for the child, to destroy him." And he rose and took the child and his mother by night, and departed to Egypt, and remained there until the death of Herod. This was to fulfill what the Lord had spoken by the prophet, "Out of Egypt have I called my son."

Then Herod, when he saw that he had been tricked by the Wise Men, was in a furious rage, and he sent and killed all the male children in Bethlehem and in all that region who were two years old or under, according to the time which he had ascertained from the Wise Men. (Matthew 2:12-16)

There you have it. How was the good news of God met? Genocide—the senseless destruction of human life. This most joyful moment in heaven was met with the murder of innocent life. And how was the Holy Family rewarded for their great faithfulness? Traveling ninety miles south in the third trimester of pregnancy. Forced to deliver the Deliverer in a cave. Having to escape to a foreign land, after a warning from an angel, under threat of death. As St. Teresa of Ávila put it so well, "If this is the way you treat your friends, Lord, no wonder you have so few of them."

Now, the skeptic (the pessimist) looks at that story and says, "You see? What kind of a God would do that to his own Son? How is that love?" The Christian (the optimist) looks at it and

praises the faithfulness of God. "Look at the lengths he goes to
for his Son: late night warnings, an angelic messenger, grace for
the journey, faithfulness in fulfilling their needs in a foreign land.
That's a loving God!"

You can tell a lot about a person by how they view the
weather. The same sky that a pessimist describes as "mostly
cloudy" an optimist calls "partly sunny." God "sends the rain
on the just and on the unjust" (Matthew 5:45). As we saw in the
last chapter, hardship doesn't mean that God doesn't love you;
he promised us times would be hard. Christianity isn't a free pass
out of the storm but a promise that you won't be swallowed up
by it. The pessimist is a navel-gazer, only seeing the world for
how it affects him; the optimist is a heaven-gazer, realizing the
only reason to take this life too seriously is if it's your only one.

## No matter how hopeless the situation looks to us, God is in control.

God's daring **rescue** mission with the flight into Egypt is more
than good storytelling or an allegory of his love. God's **rescue** of
the Holy Family is an unshakeable, unwavering reminder to us that
no matter the storm clouds that befall us, no matter the threats we
face, no matter the dangers that lurk, no matter how hopeless the
situation looks to us, God is in control. We are in God's hand; he
has, in fact, carved our names into it (Isaiah 49:16). We are always
on his mind. He knows our names (Luke 10:20).

### Promise keeper

You might be thinking, "Well, of course he's going to protect the Holy Family. Jesus is his Son. What kind of God would
just let his own Son, tiny and helpless, perish?" Exactly. May
we never doubt nor forget that we, too, are God's children, and
that our heavenly Father always keeps his promises. Read a
few for yourself: Isaiah 41:10-11, 13-14; James 4:7-8; Jeremiah
29:10-13; Psalm 111:3-5. It's been said that there are over four
thousand promises in the Bible. And what is the one thing that
God's promises all have in common? They all have the same goal:
your salvation (1 Peter 1:9).

That's how we know that God is love. That's how we can judge
if anything is truly love—if it works for our salvation. That's the
litmus test, the critical indicator in any and every relationship as
to whether someone really loves us or just says that they do. God
came not only to **rescue** us from sin but from ourselves. The late
Rich Mullins, an extraordinary Christian musician and poet, put
it this way:

> I am frightened of myself. I am frightened of the evil that I
> am capable of. I am frightened of that which You (I believe)
> would deliver me from, and yet I will not let go. . . . I think,
> Lord, that we're all afraid of the werewolves—not afraid of
> being destroyed by one—afraid of being one.[24]

We are attracted to that which we are. When we think of
ourselves as little more than products of this world—imperfect,
weak, and impure—we're drawn to (and seek out) that which we
believe to be like us. We seek that which is dirty, lifeless, finite,

and dark. Sin seeks sin. When we are freed from our sin, however, and the evil one no longer has his claws around us, the **rescue** we are praying for in "Deliver us from evil" is underway. When freed from sin, we look to remain that way. Grace seeks grace. Purity seeks purity.

## Christ uses his Church to rescue me from myself, and he does the same for you.

In asking for God's deliverance from sin, we're also asking for his deliverance from our natural, fleshly inclination to sin. We're asking Christ the surgeon to root out the cancer of our sin with the scalpel of his love. We're asking for a heart transplant—his Sacred Heart for our sinful one. We're asking for a blood transfusion, from the cross to the chalice and into our very veins. Christ accomplishes all these things through his Church on earth. Christ uses his Church to **rescue** me from myself, and he does the same for you.

### The rescue mission for wayward souls

The kingdom of heaven has an outpost on earth, a headquarters that we call the Church. Entrusted to that Church are several tools that God uses to deliver us from the evil of the world, the evil within ourselves, and all the counterfeit forms of love the devil tries to offer for our demise. To a world steeped in darkness, the Church stands as a beacon of light, calling ships out of the storm and back to the safe harbor of his mercy and love.

In the sacraments, God shouts to us in a whisper. He beckons to us, all the while veiling his grace in a way that won't make our hearts explode with love. If God didn't veil his presence in something as simple as a piece of bread, we'd likely crawl out of the church in an awe-induced daze or just drop dead on the spot. His grace is given freely for us to help insure our salvation. We encounter God's grace most tangibly, most directly, through the Church. To be clear, though, "the Church does not generate grace, grace generates the Church."[25]

God uses a number of weapons in his **rescue** mission, weapons of grace. He offers us the cross, the greatest weapon ever wielded on any battlefield. When Christ mounted the cross, he used the devil's greatest tool to defeat him; God used death to destroy death. The worst moment in history became the greatest. How beautifully paradoxical that we display the crucifix so proudly in our parishes and homes and even around our own necks, for only God can turn a torturous device of pain and death into a glorious icon of hope and life.

God didn't stop with the cross, however. He gives us many more "weapons" in our arsenal of grace. He offers us the angels and the saints. He offers us his own mother. Each of these graces points back to an encounter with him, most directly through the sacraments. The grace offered through the sacraments helps us to subdue our sinful inclinations—to keep the werewolf caged—until such time as that sinful nature is gone for good. We are reminded of the good news from St. Paul that "wherever sin increased, grace abound all the more" (Romans 5:20) and that his "grace is sufficient" for us (2 Corinthians 12:9). Grace, in turn, empowers virtue.

Virtue is free, but it does not come easy. Virtue in its most simplistic sense is a form of behavior modification. We trade in our sinful inclinations, aspiring for moral excellence. Virtue takes time. It does not occur through spontaneous bursts of our own effort but through constant exposure to and consistent receiving of God's grace. Virtue wrestles sinful whispers and evil invitations to the ground, subduing the flesh in favor of God's Spirit. Once subdued, the Lord then *co-missions* us, to work with his grace on this **rescue** mission of other souls (Matthew 28:16-20; James 5:19-20; 1 Peter 1:9).

The greatest ally we can have in this deliverance from evil is a person so "full of grace" that she is the perfection of virtue: the Blessed Mother. More than anyone else besides Christ, Mary knew the fullness of God the Father's love and trusted perfectly in his enduring promise. Mary's entire life was a living, breathing articulation of the Lord's Prayer.

### Don't mess with Mom

There is no better way to conclude this section on the "deliverance from evil" than by reflecting on our Blessed Mother, Mary. Her *fiat* signaled the end of evil as we know it. Mary's profession of faith and example of perfect trust (Luke 1:26-38) fulfilled the prophecy of Genesis (3:15), when God promised to **rescue** us with

> **We honor the Lord when we have taken his mother as our own.**

a redeemer. It was at that time that God revealed to us that the Savior would come through a woman. Mary, the new Eve, offers us a model of perfect virtue. Mary is so grace filled that her life continues to fulfill her prophecy that all generations would call her blessed (Luke 1:48). Our Church fulfills this prophecy with the greatest faithfulness, honoring Mary's discipleship by seeking her perfect intercession. We honor the Lord when we have taken his mother as our own, relishing the gift he bestowed on us with his dying breath when he told the apostle John that she is our mother as well (John 19:27).

Think about the three most important moments of Christian history: the incarnation, the passion, and Pentecost. Mary was present for all three. Her story is forever linked, not only with Christ's story, but with our own. Her life cannot be divorced from Jesus' life. Out of her love for the Father, she carried the body of Christ for nine months. Out of her love for the Son, she's been carrying the mystical body of Christ for two thousand years.

In fact, if we take a wider view of Scripture, Mary's role within salvation history "bookends" the Bible. From the beginning to the end, from the first book (Genesis 3:15) to the last (Revelation 12:1-17), the woman has been embroiled in the eternal battle of good and evil, of light and darkness. She plays an integral role in God's plan of salvation, his **rescue** mission, as he frees his children from the clutches of sin and death. Mary is one of the few people God actually "needed" to accomplish his plan. The rest of us God doesn't need, though we are immeasurably blessed that he still "wants" and "calls" us to himself (Mark 3:13).

While the Hail Mary is an utterly Scriptural prayer, a closer examination of Scripture reveals that the term "full of grace" had never been uttered before in the Old Testament. When the phrase left the lips of the angelic messenger, even Mary herself didn't fully understand the context (Luke 1:28-29). God's grace—his divine life—is living and active, constantly working for our salvation. The words spoken to Our Lady were revealing not just a moment of divine favor but the fulfillment of a centuries-old promise to God's children. The angel's proclamation of God's divine life, so present in the Blessed Virgin, was precisely the formula needed for our **rescue** from death! Mary, the New Eve, would now face evil and, allowing God to act through her *fiat*, would play an integral part in destroying death forever.

## The plan for our rescue began long before that night beneath the Bethlehem sky.

This is a **rescue** effort the likes of which humanity had never seen. The plan for our rescue began long before that night beneath the Bethlehem sky. As a pro-life Church, we know well that the journey of life begins long before birth. God conceived of the Immaculate Conception long before Mary's parents ever met. Our journey of eternal life was in the mind and heart of God from the beginning. God was working for our salvation, promising us a deliverer, planning our **rescue** from evil well before the eternal Son's delivery.

## Responding to This Petition

### Pick up the beads

God leaves nothing to chance. He is (and has been) eternally working for our salvation. He is constantly delivering us from evil. He works through all created means to offer us all that is uncreated. Mary, the crowning achievement of creation, is our greatest saint and most glorious intercessor. The Blessed Mother is the most valiant warrior against the evil one that heaven and earth have ever known. How foolish we would be if we failed to tap into this incredible source of God's grace, imploring her to wrap us in her mantle and walk with us every step of this dangerous path we call life.

If Mary plays such an indispensable role in the deliverance from evil, what makes anyone think she'd no longer figure into God's plan of deliverance? The Rosary is not merely some beads of prayer or a chain of hope—it's a weapon of grace. If you pray it already, increase your boldness in imploring others to pray it. If you haven't prayed the Rosary in a long while, dust off the beads and reignite this powerful form of prayer once again. And if you've never prayed it, ask someone to introduce you to this beautiful gift. Mary walked with Christ during his life, sufferings, and death. The perfect mother, she'll walk with us too, helping to "deliver us from evil" as she delivers our prayers to her son.

## Questions for Reflection and Discussion

1. Do you trust God implicitly, or do you struggle to trust the Father? Rate your trust on a scale of one to ten, and contemplate why you rate yourself the way you do. Did something occur in your past that is affecting your present state of trust? Explain.

2. How often do you invoke the protection or aid of your guardian angel? What does God's gift to us of angels say about God, us, the devil, and our world? Discuss.

3. When we actively seek to grow in our holiness and in our faith, the devil will do everything in his power to hinder us. What are some examples you've seen in your life of how the devil tries to impede your spiritual progress?

4. Do you ever worry that you are not strong enough to live the life that God has called you to live? If so, do you feel that fear is from God or the devil? If not, how do you avoid such doubts? Discuss.

5. Describe the role that the Blessed Virgin Mary does (or does not) play in your faith walk.

# CHAPTER 14

# "Amen"

## Strengthening Our **RESOLVE**

Over the past thirteen chapters, we have covered a lot of ground. The Lord's Prayer has taken us on a journey from earth to heaven and back to earth again. We've recalibrated our priorities and reprioritized our petitions.

So now what? How will these reflections and, more important, these timeless truths uttered within the prayer really change your life in the days to come? What do you intend to do differently with the graces God has given you for taking time out of your schedule to focus more on his prayer? What difference will this prayer make in *your* prayer life?

### Can I get an "Amen"?

What is your amen worth? What does it really mean to you? Is it a reactionary response or a response filled with **resolve**? It's interesting that we end the Lord's Prayer (and most prayers) with "Amen." The true connotation of the word carries with it an inference of action on our part. Amen is a derivative of the Hebrew word *aman*, which means "to confirm" or "to strengthen." Amen is a response of agreement and consent; amen resoundingly affirms "May it be so."

When we say "Amen," we are proclaiming, "Yes, *I believe that! I agree with that!* I profess it to be so with my whole being!"

We are professing our most strongly held beliefs. We are erupting in a chorus with our brothers and sisters, crying out the Great Amen after the consecration at Mass. We are professing "Amen" when we receive our Savior with the Eucharistic Lord. We ought to say it with intensity. We need to proclaim it with fervor. We should pray it with **resolve**.

In the Gospel of Matthew, Jesus says the word "amen" about thirty times. In the course of a normal Sunday Mass, we say or sing the word at least a dozen times. I can honestly say that most of the time when I say "amen," I'm not stopping to think about what I'm saying. I usually say it more as a reaction than a response, as a way of "ending" a prayer and moving on.

St. Paul reminded the people in Corinth:

For all the promises of God will find their yes in him. That is why we utter the Amen through him, to the glory of God. (2 Corinthians 1:20)

You see, our amen does not merely punctuate or accentuate a prayer; our amen glorifies God! The more aware we are of this fact in our hearts, the more intentional we'll be in praying "amen" with our lips, and thus the more **resolve** we'll show in glorifying God in our actions.

Jesus taught us how to pray. Jesus "the Way" gave us the way. If we believe these words that Christ entrusts to us in his prayer, this "R" Father, then our actions will follow our beliefs. Make the **resolution** to change your prayer. Schedule your week around prayer. Pray with rhythm. Read Scripture with purpose. Encounter the Eucharist, daily, with fervor. Seek mercy with urgency in the

Sacrament of Reconciliation. Prepare for the Mass early by praying the readings ahead of time. Be present to Christ throughout the day by praying the Angelus or the Liturgy of the Hours. Over one hundred Scripture passages and *Catechism* references have been parenthetically referenced in this book. If you didn't look them up during your reading, why not go back through the book and do so?

Strengthen your **resolve** to love God above all others and above all things (Mark 12:30). In all circumstances, in each daily situation, "put on love" (Colossians 3:14), not merely in words, but in loving sacrifice (Romans 12:1-2, 10; 1 Peter 2:17). Beginning in your own home and extended family, discern those whom you

> **Discern those who you need to love better, and then prayerfully ask the Lord for the help to do so.**

need to love better, and then prayerfully ask the Lord for the help to do so. Reach out in humility. Offer words of kindness and affirmation. Seek forgiveness. Look to glorify God through acts of love, remembering that opportunities for small gestures come more often than grandiose ones. Prayerfully consider your motivation in doing things for others, and your expectation—if any—for something in return. In these ways your love will be purified, and your heart will grow distinctly closer to Christ's Sacred Heart.

Another way to strengthen your daily **resolve** is to say "I do" ("Amen") by what you don't do. Fast from television, music, the newspaper, or the Internet one day a week. Get practical by sacrificing tangible, finite things to taste the beauty of the infinite in new ways.

Read about the lives of the saints and biblical heroes. Notice how one heroic life can change the world—just look at St. Francis of Assisi or Blessed Teresa of Calcutta. Notice how truly heroic people don't start out with the intention of being heroic but only with the intention of doing God's will. Saints don't desire a following; people just come, drawn not to them but to the light that radiates from and through them.

A strong **resolve** means you won't allow yourself to be swallowed, mastered, or identified by your past sins or former self. It means you claim freedom in Jesus' name and "put on Christ" (Galatians 3:27). Make the **resolution** to create more space in your mind, heart, and schedule for God's Fatherhood and relationships.

## Responding to This Petition

### *Making room for God*

Why are we so shocked when our lives get filled with stress? Why are so many Christians still so often without joy? Why is anxiety and worry more prevalent than peace in many modern believers? I'll throw out one possible answer: We don't pray enough.

Prayer is the hinge pin that holds everything else together and keeps us moving forward. Without prayer, everything falls apart. Without prayer, we're not living, we're breathing. Prayer is the most primal, most basic, and most important thing we can do as Christians. Prayer is also the very first thing we should do when we get busy.

When we don't take time to pray, we may as well be saying that it's not as high a priority as other the things in our lives that we do take time for. We often need to admit that we don't make enough time to pray.

I don't make enough time to pray, but I do make excuses. Maybe other things are pulling at me (sometimes children, literally). Maybe my prayer is interrupted, cut short, or unfocused

## Prayer is the hinge pin that holds everything else together.

because of reality—the demands of the world around me. The reality is what we call life, but that "life" is sadly no life at all. Jesus had people pulling at him. Jesus had people wanting things from him 24/7. Jesus had plenty to do. He made the time. Throughout the Scriptures we see instances when Jesus removed himself from the busyness and took time to pray. This is going to be the most obvious phrase in this book, but it needs to be said: We need to be more like Jesus.

If you drew a pie chart of your week that broke down where all of your time goes, what would it look like? When I broke down my 168-hour week, it hit me pretty hard that not enough of my time is dedicated to prayer on a daily or weekly basis. How about yours? There's probably a lot of time in there for work or school. There's definitely time in there for travel, meals, and sleep (but probably not as much as you'd like). I'll even bet that there's time for exercise or hanging out, reading, or spending time with family and friends (again, probably not as much as you'd like). None of those things is bad; each of them is good. We need relationships, activities, and rest. But God is moving *right now*. If we don't perceive it, we need to slow down.

Outside of going to Mass, how much of your time is spent with God each week? At what point did you invite God into your day? Is morning prayer the most important "meal" of your day? If you're married, do you spend more time praying together than doing tasks around the house? Are you spending more time on Facebook and less time with your face in the Book? Believe me, I'm asking myself these questions too. I feel free to ask them because I've failed at every one of them.

You've just finished an entire book dedicated to improving the way you encounter your life and your prayer through Jesus' prayer. The Spirit may have moved in your heart from time to time. You may intend to do some things differently. If so, that's great, but remember: intentions accomplish nothing if we lack **resolve**.

Part of **resolve** is the commitment to improve and the willingness to be practical. How about making a personal inventory to shed light on some areas or offer some ideas on how you might do that?

- When was the last time you got up thirty minutes early to have a cup of coffee with God in the morning?

- When was the last time you got ready for bed early, fell on your knees beside it, and really prayed before falling asleep?

- When was the last time you were able to be totally focused while praying a Rosary?

- When was the last time you fasted outside the season of Lent?

- When was the last time you read the upcoming Sunday readings a few days in advance?

- When was the last time you turned off the radio, shut off your cell phone, and invited Jesus to ride shotgun with you in your car?

- When was the last time you invited your significant other to pray with you?

- When was the last time grace before your meal took more than fifteen seconds?

- When was the last time you just opened up the *Catechism of the Catholic Church* and read a few pages?

- When was the last time you went to confession? What's keeping you from going regularly?

- When was the last time you did a spontaneous act of service for another person?

These are the questions I have begun to ask myself each week. Some weeks I'm doing great, and other weeks I fail miserably. The effort is a form of prayer, though, and demonstrates **resolve**. The reality is that I can always improve, and maybe, just maybe, you can too. Prayer isn't about words or feelings. Prayer is about time. Prayer is about presence. Prayer is about **resolve**.

If you want something you've never had, you need to be willing to do something that you've never done before. There are two things I've learned about following the Lord. First, it will never be easy. Second, it will never be boring. Now, pray the Lord's Prayer three times—slowly and intentionally—utilizing the list of the 14 "R"s below:

- Relationship
- Revelation
- Response
- Reunion
- Reverence
- Renouncement
- Reaffirmation
- Remembrance
- Reliance
- Reconciliation
- Repentance
- Reality
- Rescue
- Resolve

The disciples asked Jesus, "Teach us to pray" (Luke 11:1). Little did they realize at the time that the Lord's entire life was the Lord's Prayer. With every breath, Christ lived out these petitions in perfection. This is our path to "perfection" as well (Matthew 5:48). In these fourteen "R"s, we encounter the life of Christ. Without Christ we are not living, we are merely existing.

Our Father loves you. He doesn't just love part of you. He doesn't just love the parts of you that you love. He loves all of you, and he is a jealous God who won't settle for one part of your heart. He doesn't want to dwell in one area of your life or spend time with you just one day a week. He wants all of you. He's coming for you. He wants to bless you. He wants to heal you. He wants to give you heaven. Your life is your response to this invitation.

Become a child again. In your prayer, crawl up on our heavenly Father's lap and let him love you. Responding to our Father in this way proclaims him far more than words ever could.

Amen?

# Notes

1. Peter Kreeft, *Fundamentals of the Faith: Essays in Christian Apologetics* (San Francisco: Ignatius Press, 1988), 189.

2. Christopher Cuddy and Mark Hart, *Sword of the Spirit: A Beginner's Guide to St. Paul* (Mesa, AZ: Life Teen, 2008), 31.

3. Walt Mueller, *Youth Culture 101* (Grand Rapids, MI: Zondervan, 2007), 45.

4. Scott Hahn, *Understanding Our Father: Biblical Reflections on the Lord's Prayer* (Steubenville, OH: Emmaus Road Publishing, 2002), 10.

5. Max Lucado, *The Great House of God* (Nashville, TN: Word Publishing Group, 1997), 14.

6. Fyodor Dostoevsky, *The Brothers Karamazov* (Penguin Classics, 1982), 375.

7. R. C. Sproul, *The Holiness of God* (Carol Stream, IL: Tyndale House Publishers, 1985), 138.

8. Hahn, *Understanding Our Father*, 21.

9.  Ibid., 17.

10.  Joseph Ratzinger (Pope Benedict XVI), *Jesus of Nazareth* (New York: Doubleday, 2007), 149.

11.  Ibid., 149.

12.  N.T. Wright, *Following Jesus* (Grand Rapids, MI: William B. Eerdmans Publishing Company, 1994), 9.

13.  Ibid., 9.

14.  Pope Benedict XVI, *Deus Caritas Est*, 12.

15.  Mark Hart, *T3: The Lion and the Lamb* (West Chester, PA: Ascension Press), 4.

16.  Raneiro Cantalamessa, *Mary: Mirror of the Church* (Collegeville, MN: The Liturgical Press, 1992), 196.

17.  Hahn, *Understanding Our Father*, 43.

18.  G. K. Chesterton, *Why I Am a Catholic* (San Francisco: Ignatius Press, 1990), 127.

19.  Mark Hart, *Ask the Bible Geek 2: More Answers to Questions from Catholic Teens* (Cincinnati, OH: Servant Books, 2006), 103.

20. Mark Hart, *Come Clean: A Teen Guide to Reconciliation* (Mesa, AZ: Life Teen, 2009), 31.

21. Hahn, *Understanding Our Father*, 53.

22. Francis Fernandez Carvajal, *Lukewarmness: The Devil in Disguise* (New York: Scepter Publishers, 1992).

23. Matthias Scheeben, *The Glories of Divine Grace* (Rockford, IL: TAN Books, 2000), 280.

24. James Bryan Smith, *Rich Mullins: An Arrow Pointing to Heaven* (Nashville, TN: Broadman & Holman Publishers, 2000), 135.

25. Raneiro Cantalamessa, *Mary: Mirror of the Church*, 30.

# the WORD among us®
### The *Spirit* of Catholic Living

This book was published by The Word Among Us. For nearly thirty years, The Word Among Us has been answering the call of the Second Vatican Council to help Catholic laypeople encounter Christ in the Scriptures—a call reiterated recently by Pope Benedict XVI and a Synod of Bishops.

The name of our company comes from the prologue to the Gospel of John and reflects the vision and purpose of all of our publications: to be an instrument of the Spirit, whose desire is to manifest Jesus' presence in and to the children of God. In this way, we hope to contribute to the church's ongoing mission of proclaiming the gospel to the world and growing ever more deeply in our love for the Lord.

Our monthly devotional magazine, *The Word Among Us*, features meditations on the daily and Sunday Mass readings, and currently reaches more than one million Catholics in North America each year and another 500,000 Catholics in 100 countries. Our press division has published nearly 180 books and Bible studies over the past ten years.

To learn more about who we are and what we publish, log on to our Web site at **www.wau.org**. There you will find a variety of Catholic resources that will help you grow in your faith.

# Embrace His Word, Listen to God . . .

www.wau.org